EXCEL MASTERY 2026

FROM BEGINNER TO EXPERT

THE COMPLETE GUIDE TO FORMULAS, FUNCTIONS, AND REAL-WORLD APPLICATIONS

TABLE OF CONTENTS

INTRODUCTION

Welcome to the world of Microsoft Excel, the ultimate tool for organizing, analyzing, and visualizing data. Whether you're a beginner looking to grasp the basics or an advanced user ready to tackle complex tasks, this book is your comprehensive guide to mastering Excel.

Excel is more than just a spreadsheet program—it's a powerhouse that transforms raw data into actionable insights. From tracking personal budgets to managing business operations, Excel is a go-to solution for millions of users worldwide. Its versatility spans industries, professions, and hobbies, making it an essential skill for students, professionals, and lifelong learners alike.

I.   WHY EXCEL MATTERS

In today's data-driven world, knowing how to use Excel is not just an advantage—it's a necessity. Employers often rank Excel expertise among the top skills they look for in candidates. Beyond the workplace, Excel can help you simplify daily life, whether you're planning an event, tracking your fitness goals, or organizing family expenses.

II.   WHAT EXCEL CAN DO

Excel is more than just rows and columns—it's a versatile tool that can handle a wide range of tasks, from simple to much more complicated spreadsheets and reporting.

- **Organize Information**: Keep track of personal budgets, to-do lists, inventories, or schedules with structured and customizable spreadsheets.
- **Perform Calculations**: Use formulas and functions to solve mathematical problems, calculate statistics, or project financial forecasts with ease.
- **Visualize Data**: Turn numbers into meaningful insights with charts, graphs, and sparklines, making your data easier to understand and present.
- **Analyze Trends**: Uncover patterns and insights with tools like pivot tables, conditional formatting, and filters, whether you're working on sales data or survey results.
- **Automate Tasks**: Save time by automating repetitive tasks with macros and built-in tools like Flash Fill.
- **Collaborate Seamlessly**: Share and edit files in real-time with colleagues or friends using OneDrive and Teams integration.
- **Manage Projects**: Track progress, monitor deadlines, and organize tasks with customized templates tailored to your needs.

With its features and capabilities, you can use Excel in both your personal and professional life.

1. IN THE WORKPLACE

Budget Management: A small business owner uses Excel to track income and expenses, create profit and loss statements, and plan for future growth.

Project Tracking: A project manager keeps track of deadlines, milestones, and team responsibilities using Excel's templates and Gantt charts.

Sales Analysis: A salesperson analyzes monthly sales figures with pivot tables to identify top-performing products and forecast trends.

Data Reporting: A marketing analyst creates dashboards with charts and graphs to present campaign performance to stakeholders.

2. IN PERSONAL LIFE

Household Budgeting: Manage monthly income, expenses, and savings goals in a simple and customizable spreadsheet.

Event Planning: Plan a wedding or birthday party by keeping track of guest lists, seating arrangements, and budgets.

Fitness Tracking: Monitor weight, diet, and exercise progress over time using Excel's visualization tools.

Educational Planning: A student uses Excel to organize study schedules, track grades, and calculate GPA.

Excel adapts to your goals, whether you're crunching numbers at work, organizing your personal life, or exploring hobbies. With its powerful tools and endless possibilities, it's no wonder Excel is the go-to application for millions of users worldwide.

III. WHAT YOU'LL LEARN IN THIS BOOK

This book is designed to take you on a journey through Excel, starting with the fundamentals and advancing to powerful features that will save you time and effort. You'll learn how to:

- Navigate the Excel interface and understand its key components.
- Create and format spreadsheets for professional and personal use.
- Use formulas and functions to perform calculations and analyze data.
- Visualize information with charts, graphs, and sparklines.
- Collaborate with others using cloud-based tools like OneDrive.

Each chapter is packed with step-by-step instructions, real-world examples, and practical exercises to reinforce your learning. Whether you're a student trying to ace a project, a business owner managing finances, or a hobbyist organizing your passions, there's something in this book for you.

IV. WHO THIS BOOK IS FOR

This book caters to a wide range of readers:

- **Beginners** who want to learn Excel from the ground up.
- **Intermediate users** looking to sharpen their skills and discover new features.
- **Advanced users** ready to explore advanced techniques like Power Query and VBA.
- Anyone who wants to save time, improve efficiency, and unlock Excel's full potential.

V. HOW TO USE THIS BOOK

To make the most of this book, start at the beginning and progress through each chapter. The content is structured to build on what you've learned, but you can also jump to specific sections that interest you. Don't just read—try the exercises, experiment with the tools, and apply what you've learned to your own projects. By the end of this book, you'll be confident and ready to handle any Excel challenge.

VI. LET'S GET STARTED

It's time to roll up your sleeves and dive into Excel. Whether you're solving problems, uncovering patterns, or simplifying workflows, Excel will become your trusted companion. Let this book be your guide as you explore its incredible possibilities. Ready to begin? Let's unlock the power of Excel together!

CHAPTER 1:
GETTING STARTED WITH EXCEL

I. INSTALLING AND LAUNCHING EXCEL

Excel is one of the most widely used tools in the Microsoft Office suite, and setting it up is the first step toward unlocking its powerful features. Whether you're new to Excel or setting it up on a new device, follow this guide to ensure a smooth installation and launch process.

1. INSTALLING EXCEL

i. Through Microsoft 365 Subscription:

If you have a Microsoft 365 subscription, Excel comes as part of the suite. To install:

1. Log in to your Microsoft account at www.office.com.
2. Navigate to **"Install Office"** and select the suite appropriate for your device.
3. Download the installer and follow the on-screen instructions.
4. During installation, ensure you have a stable internet connection.

ii. Through a Standalone License:

If you have purchased Excel as a standalone product:

1. Enter the product key at www.office.com/setup.
2. Follow the instructions to download and install Excel.

2. LAUNCHING EXCEL

Once installed, launching Excel is simple and varies slightly depending on your device.

i. On Windows:
1. Click the **Start Menu** and type "Excel" into the search bar.
2. Select the Excel application from the results to open it.

ii. On macOS:
1. Open the **Applications** folder and locate Microsoft Excel.
2. Double-click the Excel icon to launch the application.

3. FIRST-TIME SETUP

When you launch Excel for the first time, you may encounter the following setup steps:

1. **Sign In:** Enter your Microsoft account credentials to activate the product.
2. **Choose Your Theme:** Select your preferred color theme for the Excel interface (default, dark, or colorful).
3. **Explore Tutorials:** Excel may offer a quick walkthrough of its features. This can be skipped or explored depending on your familiarity with the tool.

4. QUICK TIPS FOR A SMOOTH START

- **Pin Excel to Your Taskbar:** Right-click the Excel icon after launching it and select **"Pin to Taskbar"** for quick access.
- **Ensure Updates:** Regularly update Excel via the Microsoft 365 app or your device's app store to access the latest features and security enhancements.

Once installed, you're ready to dive into Excel's interface and start creating your first workbook.

II. EXPLORING THE EXCEL INTERFACE: WORKSHEETS, RIBBON, AND WORKBOOKS

When you launch Excel, the Excel Start Screen will be the first thing you see.

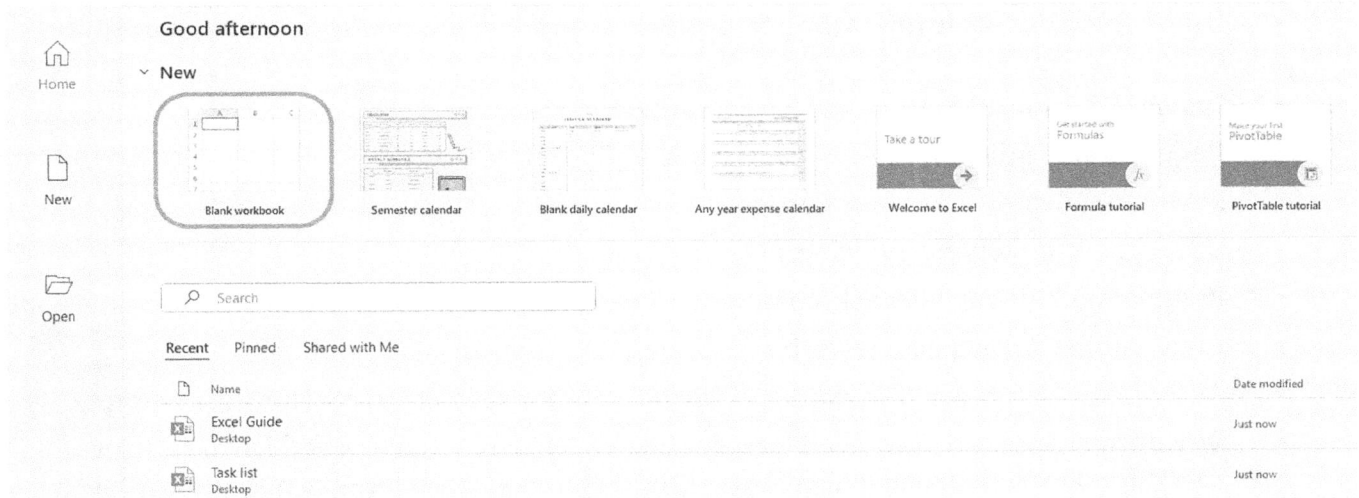

Chapter 1 - Figure 1.   Excel Start Screen.jpg

To begin working in Excel, locate and click "Blank Workbook" on the Start Screen. This action will take you to the main Excel interface, where you can start creating or editing your data.

WHAT IS A WORKBOOK?

A workbook is the file format used in Microsoft Excel, consisting of one or more worksheets (commonly called spreadsheets). Each workbook is assigned a default name, such as Sheet1,

Sheet2, or Sheet3, depending on the number of new worksheets added.

Chapter 1 - Figure 1 illustrates a blank workbook as it appears upon opening Excel. Take a moment to familiarize yourself with the layout and tools. Note that the appearance of your screen may vary slightly depending on the version of Excel you are using.

1.   KEY COMPONENTS OF THE EXCEL INTERFACE

When you open Excel, you are greeted by its default layout. Each element serves a unique purpose to help you interact with and manage data seamlessly.

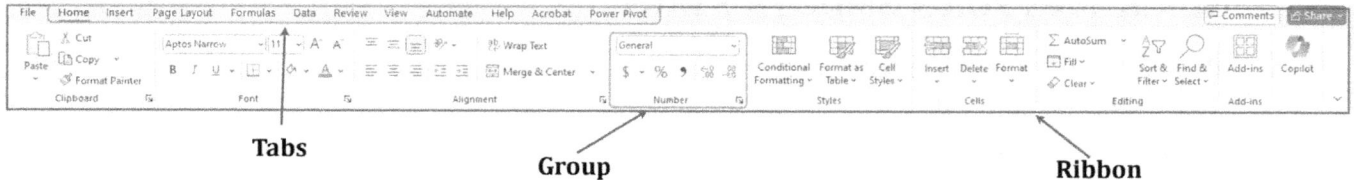

Tabs   **Group**   **Ribbon**

Chapter 1 - Figure 2.   Excel Interface New.png

i.   The Ribbon

The ribbon is located at the top of the Excel window and organizes tools into tabs and groups.

TABS:

- **Home**: Includes basic formatting tools (font, alignment, number formatting) and editing options.
- **Insert**: Lets you add charts, tables, pictures, and more.
- **Page Layout**: Adjust margins, orientation, and printing settings.
- **Formulas**: Access functions, formula auditing tools, and calculation settings.
- **Data**: Tools for sorting, filtering, and importing data.
- **Review**: Includes spell check, comments, and accessibility tools.
- **View**: Adjust worksheet views, freeze panes, and show or hide gridlines.
- **Automate**: Allows you to record and run automations using TypeScript-based scripts.
- **Developer**: Access to advanced features like VBA macros, ActiveX and Form controls, and XML commands. Some advanced Developer features in Excel for Mac may differ slightly from the Windows version.
- **Help**: Provides quick access to the Help Task Pane and allows you to contact Microsoft support, send feedback, and view training videos.

If you're using Microsoft 365, you'll see a Copilot button on the right side of the Home tab. Copilot is Microsoft's AI assistant that can help explain formulas, summarize data, suggest charts, and perform other tasks. A chapter later in the book will show how to use Copilot effectively.

GROUPS:

Each tab is divided into logical groups. For example, in the **Home** tab, you'll find groups like Clipboard, Font, Alignment, and Number.

ii. Worksheets

- **Worksheet**: Each Excel file (aka workbook) consists of individual worksheets, visible as tabs at the bottom of the screen. By default, Excel starts with one worksheet, but you can add or delete them as needed.

iii. Rows, Columns, and Cells

- **Rows**: Numbered sequentially along the left side (1, 2, 3...).
- **Columns**: Lettered alphabetically across the top (A, B, C...).
- **Cells**: The intersection of a row and a column (e.g., A1, B2) is called a cell, where data is entered.

iv. Formula Bar

- Located above the worksheet grid, the formula bar shows the content or formula of the selected cell. You use it to enter or edit data and formulas.

v. Name Box

- Found to the left of the formula bar, the name box displays the address of the currently selected cell (e.g., A1).
- You can also use it to navigate to specific cells or ranges.

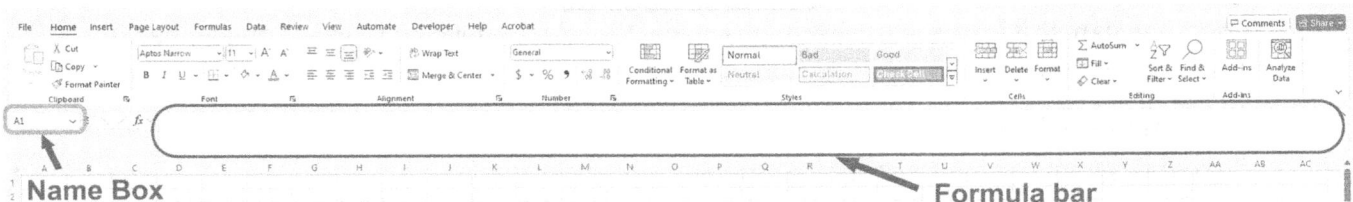

Chapter 1 - Figure 3.   Formula Bar and Name Box.jpg

vi. Status Bar

- Found at the bottom of the Excel window, it provides quick information about selected data, such as averages, sums, and counts.
- You can customize the status bar to show useful tools like Zoom Slider and View Options.

vii. Quick Access Toolbar

- Located above or below the ribbon, this toolbar provides shortcuts for frequently used commands like Save, Undo, and Redo. You can customize it to include other commands you use often.

viii. Sheet Tabs and Navigation Buttons

- The bottom left of the interface shows the sheet tabs in a workbook.
- Navigation buttons allow you to scroll through sheets when you have more tabs than can be displayed.

ix. View Options

- Located in the bottom-right corner, these options let you toggle between Normal, Page Layout, and Page Break Preview views.
- Use the Zoom Slider to adjust the magnification of the worksheet.

Chapter 1 - Figure 4.   Status Bar, Quick Access ToolBar and Sheet Tabs.jpg

2.   HOW TO NAVIGATE THE EXCEL INTERFACE

i.   Showing the Ribbon in Excel

If the ribbon has vanished from your Excel interface, there's no need to worry. You can easily restore it using the methods below:

- Pressing **Ctrl + F1** to toggle the ribbon on or off.
- Double-clicking on any ribbon tab to expand it.
- Right-clicking any ribbon tab and deselecting **Collapse the Ribbon** (Excel 2019 - 2013) or **Minimize the Ribbon** (Excel 2010 and 2007).
- Clicking any tab temporarily to display the ribbon. In Excel 2016 and 2019, click the small **pin icon** in the lower-right corner to keep the ribbon always visible.

ii.   Hiding the Ribbon in Excel

If the ribbon takes up too much space on your screen, especially on smaller laptops, you can collapse it to show only the tab names or hide it entirely.

1.   **Collapse the Ribbon**:

- Press **Ctrl + F1**, the quickest way to hide the ribbon.

- Double-click an active tab to collapse the ribbon.
- Click the **up arrow** in the ribbon's lower-right corner.

2. **Full Ribbon Disappearance**:

If the entire ribbon vanishes, Excel might have switched to full-screen mode. Restore it by:

- Clicking the **...** to temporarily display the ribbon, then clicking **Ribbon Display Options** button in the top-right corner of the Excel window.
- Selecting **Always show Ribbon** to bring back the ribbon permanently.

iii. Common Ribbon Issues and Fixes

1. **Tabs Appear, but Commands Have Disappeared**:

Press **Ctrl + F1** or double-click any ribbon tab to re-display commands.

2. **Contextual Tabs Missing**:

If object-specific tabs (e.g., for charts, images, or PivotTables) are not visible, click the object to bring the tabs back into focus.

3. **Add-ins Tab Missing**:

If an add-in tab (e.g., for an Excel extension) disappears, Excel might have disabled the add-in.

- Navigate to **File > Excel Options > Add-ins > Disabled Items > Go**.
- Select the add-in and click **Enable** to restore it.

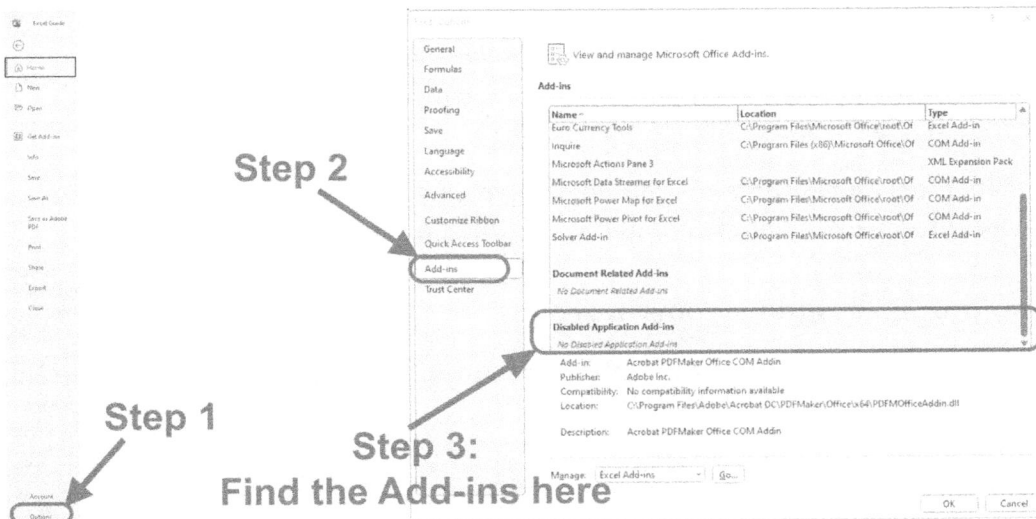

Chapter 1 - Figure 5.   Enable Add-ins.jpg

iv. Customizing the Ribbon in Excel

Personalizing the ribbon can make your workflow more efficient by putting frequently used commands at your fingertips.

1. **Access the Customize Ribbon Window**:

Right-click the ribbon and choose Customize the Ribbon from the context menu. In the Customize Ribbon window, you can create custom tabs and groups, add or remove commands, show, hide, or rename tabs and rearrange tabs and groups.

2. **Enabling Hidden Tabs**:

Some tabs, like the **Developer Tab**, are not displayed by default. To enable it:

- Right-click the ribbon and choose **Customize the Ribbon**.
- Under **Main Tabs**, check the **Developer** option and click **OK**.

Similarly, activate other hidden tabs like the **Draw Tab** using the same process.

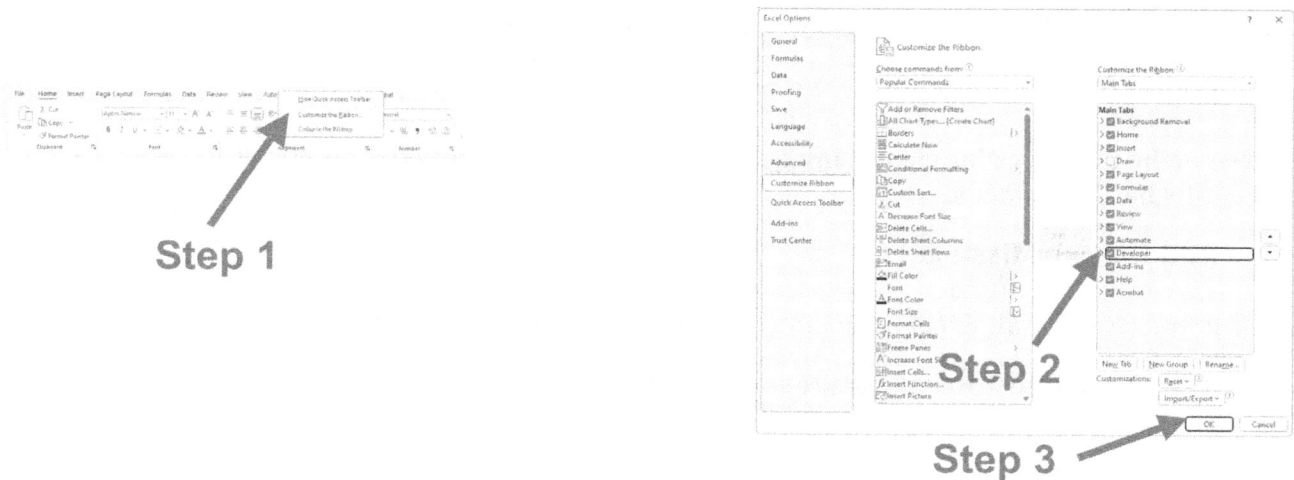

Chapter 1 - Figure 6.   Enable Hidden Tabs.jpg

v.   Accessing Hidden Tools in Groups

Excel organizes its tools and commands into logical groups within each tab of the ribbon. However, not all available tools in a group are immediately visible on the ribbon.

Here's how you can access hidden tools in groups.

1. **Locate the Group**: Identify the ribbon group (e.g., Font or Alignment on the Home tab).

2. **Find the Dialog Box Launcher**: Look for the small diagonal arrow in the group's bottom-right corner.

3. **Open the Dialog Box**: Click the arrow to reveal advanced options and settings.

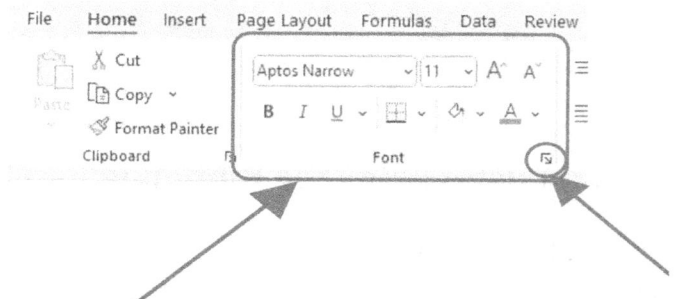

III. UNDERSTANDING ROWS, COLUMNS, AND CELLS

Rows, columns, and cells are the fundamental building blocks of any Excel worksheet. Mastering their structure and functionality will allow you to efficiently organize, input, and analyze data.

1. WHAT ARE ROWS, COLUMNS, AND CELLS?

i. Rows:

- Rows are horizontal lines of data and are numbered sequentially along the left side of the worksheet (e.g., 1, 2, 3…).
- A worksheet in Excel can have up to 1,048,576 rows.

ii. Columns:

- Columns are vertical lines of data and are labeled alphabetically across the top of the worksheet (e.g., A, B, C…).
- After column Z, Excel continues labeling columns as AA, AB, AC, and so on, with a total of 16,384 columns.

iii. Cells:

- A cell is the intersection of a row and a column, forming a single box in the worksheet grid. Each cell is identified by its **cell reference** (e.g., A1 for the cell in column A, row 1).
- Cells are the primary units where you enter data, formulas, and functions.

2. NAVIGATING ROWS, COLUMNS, AND CELLS

i. Selecting Rows and Columns:

- To select a row, click on its number on the left side of the worksheet.
- To select a column, click on its letter at the top of the worksheet.

ii. Moving Between Cells:

- Use the arrow keys on your keyboard to move up, down, left, or right.
- Press **Tab** to move to the next cell on the right, and press **Shift + Tab** to move to the cell on the left.
- Press **Enter** to move down to the next cell in a column, and **Shift + Enter** to move up.

iii. Selecting Multiple Cells:

- Click and drag your mouse to select a range of cells.
- Use **Shift + Arrow Keys** to expand the selection.
- To select non-adjacent cells, hold **Ctrl** while clicking the cells you want.

3. USING ROWS, COLUMNS, AND CELLS

i. Entering Data:

- Click on a cell and start typing to enter data.
- Press **Enter** or click another cell to confirm the entry.

ii. Adjusting Row Height and Column Width:

- Hover over the boundary between row numbers or column letters until the cursor changes to a double arrow. Drag to resize.
- Double-click the boundary to auto-adjust to fit the content.
- In the Home tab, go to group Cells and select **Format**. From there, you can precisely enter the desired width and height of selected cells, or select AutoFit for width and height.

iii. Inserting and Deleting Rows or Columns:

- Right-click on a row number or column letter and select **Insert** to add a new row or column.
- Select **Delete** from the same menu to remove rows or columns.

iv. Merging and Splitting Cells:

- Use the **Merge & Center** option in the Home tab to combine multiple cells into one.
- To split merged cells, select the merged cell and click **Merge & Center** again to unmerge.

4. TIPS FOR WORKING WITH ROWS, COLUMNS, AND CELLS

i. Jump to a Specific Cell:

- Use the **Name Box** (next to the formula bar) to type a cell reference (e.g., E5) and press **Enter** to navigate directly to it.

ii. Highlight Entire Rows or Columns:

- Click the row number or column letter to highlight the entire row or column.

iii. Use Shortcuts for Efficiency:

- Select an entire row: **Shift + Space**.
- Select an entire column: **Ctrl + Space**.

IV. CREATING AND SAVING YOUR FIRST WORKBOOK

Creating and saving your first workbook is a fundamental step in using Excel. A workbook is the primary file type in Excel, and it consists of one or more worksheets where you can input, calculate, and analyze data. This section will guide you through the process of creating, naming, and saving your first workbook.

1. CREATING A NEW WORKBOOK

i. From the Start Screen:

1. Launch Excel. The **Excel Start Screen** will appear.
2. Click **Blank Workbook** to create a new workbook with a single blank worksheet (See Figure 1).

ii. From Within Excel:

1. Go to **File > New**.
2. Select **Blank Workbook** or choose a template if you need a pre-designed layout.

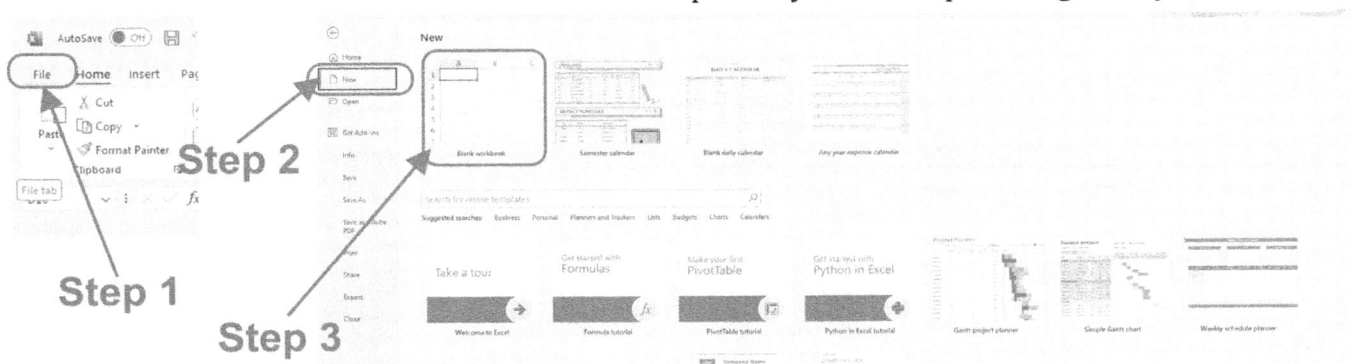

Chapter 1 - Figure 7. *Create a new workbook.jpg*

2. SAVING YOUR WORKBOOK

Once you've created your workbook, saving it ensures your work isn't lost and allows you to reopen it later.

i. Saving for the First Time:

1. Click **File > Save As**.
2. Choose a location to save your workbook:

   - **This PC** for local storage.
   - **OneDrive** for cloud storage.

3. Enter a file name in the **File Name** field.
4. Select a file format:

   - **Excel Workbook (*.xlsx)**: The default file type.
   - **Excel Macro-Enabled Workbook (*.xlsm)**: For workbooks containing macros.
   - **CSV (Comma Delimited)**: For simple text-based data files.

5. Click **Save**.

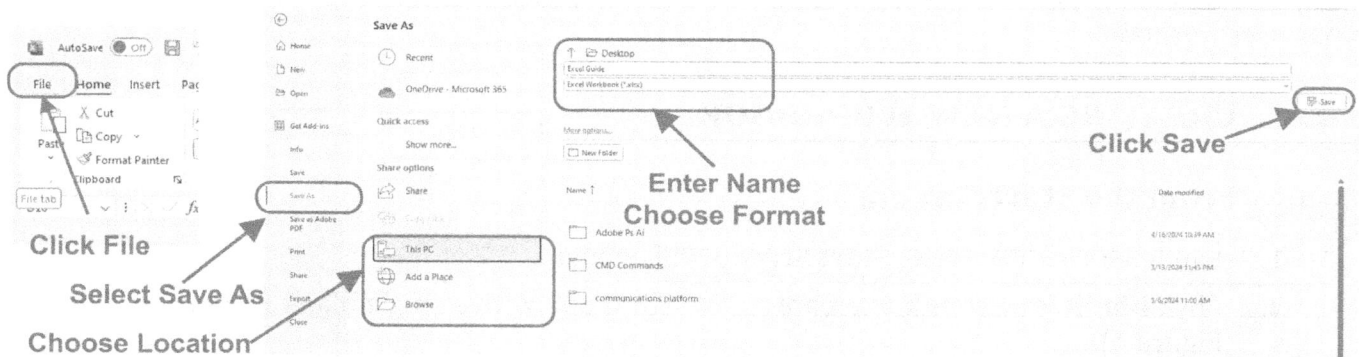

Chapter 1 - Figure 8.   Save a Workbook.jpg

ii. Quick Saving:

- Click the **Save** icon on the Quick Access Toolbar (floppy disk icon).
- Use the shortcut **Ctrl + S** to quickly save your work.

iii. AutoSave:

If you're using OneDrive or SharePoint, enable **AutoSave** at the top-left corner of the Excel window. This feature automatically saves changes in real-time.

3. OPENING SAVED WORKBOOKS

To access a saved workbook:

1. Go to **File > Open**.
2. Select the location where the workbook is saved (e.g., Recent, This PC, or OneDrive).
3. Browse and click on the file to open it.

V. EXCEL TERMINOLOGY

To work effectively in Excel, it's essential to understand its core terminology. These foundational terms will help you navigate the application and make the most of its features. Let's explore the key concepts of Excel.

1. CELLS

A **cell** is the basic building block of an Excel worksheet, where data is entered. Each cell is identified by a unique **cell reference** based on its column and row (e.g., **A1** refers to the cell in column A, row 1).

Active Cell: The currently selected cell is outlined, and its reference is displayed in the **Name Box**.

2.   RANGES

A **range** is a selection of two or more cells, identified by the references of the top-left and bottom-right cells separated by a colon (e.g., **A1:B5**). Ranges can span across rows, columns, or both.

3.   FORMULAS

Formulas perform calculations or operations in Excel. They always begin with an **equals sign (=)**. A formula can include:

- **Operators**: Arithmetic symbols like +, -, *, and /.
- **Cell References**: To use data from specific cells in the calculation.
- **Functions**: Predefined formulas in Excel.

4.   FUNCTIONS

Functions are built-in formulas that simplify complex calculations. Each function has a specific name and syntax.

- **AVERAGE**: Calculates the average of selected numbers.
- **IF**: Performs a logical test and returns one value for TRUE and another for FALSE.
- **VLOOKUP**: Finds values in a table based on a lookup value.
- **CONCATENATE** (or **TEXTJOIN**): Combines text from multiple cells.

5.   CHARTS

Charts visually represent data in a worksheet, making it easier to analyze and interpret. Excel offers several types of charts, including:

- **Column Charts**: Display data as vertical bars.
- **Pie Charts**: Show proportions of a whole.
- **Line Charts**: Highlight trends over time.
- **Scatter Plots**: Show relationships between variables.

6.   OTHERS

- Dynamic Arrays: Excel formulas that automatically spill results into multiple cells (e.g., FILTER, SORT, UNIQUE). You'll learn these in later chapters.
- Copilot Prompts: Short instructions you type into Excel Copilot to ask it to create formulas, clean data, or summarize information.

Understanding Excel terminology will make navigating the software intuitive and efficient. Whether you're performing calculations, formatting data, or creating visualizations, these concepts are the building blocks for success in Excel.

CHAPTER 2: BASIC EXCEL SKILLS

Excel's true power begins with mastering its basic skills. In this chapter, you'll learn how to enter and format data effectively, manage worksheets, and use essential formulas like SUM, AVERAGE, and COUNT. Additionally, you'll explore time-saving tools like AutoFill and Flash Fill, and gain insights into saving and printing your workbooks. These foundational skills will set you up for success as you dive deeper into Excel's capabilities.

I.   ENTERING AND FORMATTING DATA

1.   ENTERING DATA

Data entry in Excel involves typing or importing information into cells. This can include text, numbers, dates, and formulas.

Entering Text: click on the cell where you want to add text, then type your text and press **Enter** or click another cell to confirm. Excel automatically left-aligns text in cells.

Entering Numbers: numbers can be input directly into a cell. Excel aligns numbers to the right by default. Use the **Number Format** options to format numbers as currency, percentages, or dates.

Entering Dates: type the date in a recognized format (e.g., 12/31/2024). Excel stores dates as serial numbers, allowing for calculations and sorting.

Editing Data: double-click a cell to edit its contents directly or press **F2** to enter edit mode for the active cell.

2.   FORMATTING DATA

Formatting improves the visual presentation of your data, making it easier to interpret.

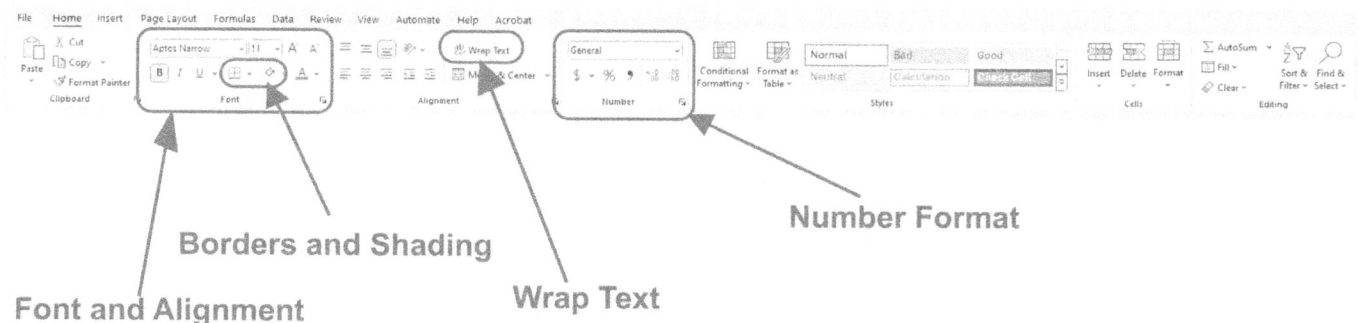

Number Format

Borders and Shading

Font and Alignment

Wrap Text

Chapter 2 - Figure 9.   Format Data.jpg

- **Font and Alignment:** select a cell or range of cells, then use the **Home** tab to change:
  - » Font type, size, and color.
  - » Bold, italic, or underline text.
  - » Align text to the left, center, or right.
- **Cell Borders and Shading:**
  - » Add borders by selecting cells and clicking the **Borders** icon in the **Home** tab.
  - » Apply shading using the **Fill Color** tool to highlight specific cells.
- **Number Formatting:** use the **Number** group in the Home tab to apply:
  - » General: Default format for numbers.
  - » Number: Displays numbers with decimals.
  - » Currency: Adds a currency symbol (e.g., $).
  - » Percentage: Converts numbers into percentages.
  - » Date: Formats data into date styles (e.g., MM/DD/YYYY).
- **Wrap Text:** use the **Wrap Text** option in the Home tab to display long text within a single cell without spilling into adjacent cells.
- **Centralize data among cells without merging:** select the cells, then:
  - » Go to **Home > Format > Format Cells** or press **Ctrl + 1**.
  - » In the **Alignment** tab, set **Horizontal** to **Center Across Selection** and click **OK**.
    The header will be centered, and you can still select individual columns (Ctrl + Space).

3. CLEARING AND DELETING DATA

- **Clearing Content:** select the cell or range and press **Delete** to remove its content.
- **Clearing Formatting:** use **Home > Clear > Clear Formats** to remove all applied formatting while keeping the data intact.
- **Deleting Cells:** right-click a cell or range and choose **Delete**, then select how to shift the surrounding cells.

4. TIPS FOR EFFECTIVE DATA ENTRY AND FORMATTING

- **Use Consistent Formatting:** consistent fonts, colors, and alignments make your worksheet easier to read.
- **Apply Cell Styles:** use pre-designed styles in **Home > Styles** for a professional look.
- **Leverage Shortcuts:**
  - » **Ctrl + 1**: Open the Format Cells dialog box.
  - » **Ctrl + Shift + $**: Apply currency format.
  - » **Ctrl + Shift + %**: Apply percentage format.

II. MANAGING WORKSHEETS: ADDING, RENAMING, AND DELETING

Worksheets are individual pages within an Excel workbook where you store and organize your data. Managing worksheets effectively is essential for organizing complex data sets or projects across multiple sheets.

1. ADDING WORKSHEETS

By default, a new workbook starts with one worksheet, but you can add as many as you need.

- **Using the New Sheet Button:** click the **"+" icon** (located next to the sheet tabs at the bottom) to add a new worksheet. The new sheet is named sequentially (e.g., Sheet2, Sheet3).

- **Using the Ribbon:** go to the **Home** tab, navigate to the **Cells** group, and click **Insert > Insert Sheet**.

- **Using Keyboard Shortcuts:** press **Shift + F11** to quickly insert a new worksheet.

Option 1
Click on "+" icon

Option 2: Home tab > Cells group > Insert > Insert Sheet

Option 3: Shift + F11

Chapter 2 - Figure 10.   Adding worksheet.jpg

2. RENAMING WORKSHEETS

Giving worksheets meaningful names makes your workbook easier to navigate.

- **Renaming via Double-Click:** double-click the sheet tab at the bottom of the Excel window. Type the new name and press **Enter**.

- **Renaming via Right-Click:** right-click the sheet tab you want to rename. Select **Rename** from the menu, type the new name, and press **Enter**.

- **Naming Best Practices:** use descriptive names (e.g., "Sales_Data" or "Expense_Report"). Avoid special characters and keep names short for better readability.

3. DELETING WORKSHEETS

If you no longer need a worksheet, you can remove it from your workbook.

- **Deleting via Right-Click:** right-click the sheet tab you want to delete. Select **Delete** from the context menu.

- **Deleting via Ribbon:** go to the **Home** tab, navigate to the **Cells** group, and click **Delete > Delete Sheet**.

Precautions: Excel will prompt you to confirm the deletion if the sheet contains data. Once deleted, the action cannot be undone, so double-check before proceeding.

4. REARRANGING WORKSHEETS

Organizing the order of your worksheets can make navigation more intuitive.

- **Reordering Tabs**: click and drag the sheet tab to a new position in the row of tabs.
- **Grouping Worksheets**: hold **Ctrl** and click on multiple sheet tabs to group them. Actions performed on one sheet (e.g., formatting) while the grouped sheets are selected will apply to all of them.

5. HIDING AND UNHIDING WORKSHEETS

To declutter your workbook without deleting data, you can hide unnecessary worksheets.

- **Hiding a Worksheet**: right-click the sheet tab and select **Hide**.
- **Unhiding a Worksheet**: right-click any sheet tab and select **Unhide**.
  - » In the dialog box, choose the hidden sheet you want to unhide and click **OK**.

6. TIPS FOR MANAGING WORKSHEETS

- **Use Tab Colors**: right-click a sheet tab, select **Tab Color**, and choose a color to visually organize your workbook.
- **Duplicate Worksheets**: right-click a sheet tab, select **Move or Copy**, and check **Create a Copy** to duplicate the sheet.
- **Limit Worksheet Clutter**: avoid adding unnecessary sheets and keep your workbook concise for easy navigation.

Managing worksheets effectively ensures your workbook is structured and easy to use, even when handling large datasets or complex projects. In the next section, we'll explore working with basic formulas like SUM, AVERAGE, and COUNT to perform essential calculations.

III. WORKING WITH BASIC FORMULAS (SUM, AVERAGE, COUNT)

1. USING THE SUM FUNCTION

The **SUM** function adds values in a range of cells.

- **Syntax**:
  =SUM(number 1, number 2,...)
- **Understand the arguments**:
  - » The number1, number2, ...: These are the arguments representing the numbers you want to add. You can input up to 255 arguments.

» The arguments can be individual numbers, cell references, ranges, or a combination of these.

- **Steps to Use SUM**:
  » Click on the cell where you want the result.

  » Type =SUM(and select the range of cells you want to add, or select the cells you want to add.

  » Press **Enter** to calculate the total.

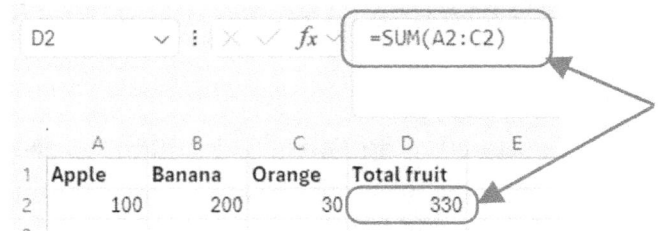

Quick Tip: Use the **AutoSum** button in the **Home** tab or on the ribbon to quickly sum a selected range. Shortcut for this AutoSum is Alt + =.

2. USING THE AVERAGE FUNCTION

The **AVERAGE** function calculates the mean of a range of values.

- **Syntax**:
  =AVERAGE(Number 1, Number 2,...)

- **Understand the arguments**:
  » The number1, number2, ...: These are the arguments representing the numbers you want to add. You can input up to 255 arguments.

  » The arguments can be individual numbers, cell references, ranges, or a combination of these.

- **Steps to Use AVERAGE:**
  » Select the cell where you want the result.

  » Type =AVERAGE(and highlight the range of cells or select the cells you want to calculate average of.

  » Press **Enter** to compute.

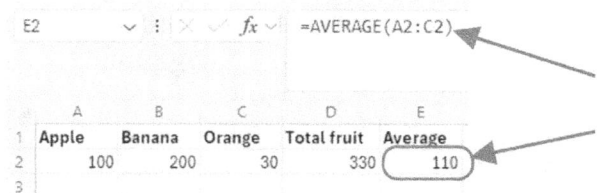

3. USING THE COUNT FUNCTION

The **COUNT** function counts the number of numeric entries in a range of cells.

- **Syntax**:
  =COUNT(value 1, [value 2],...)

- **Understand the arguments**:
  » The value1, value2, ...: These are the arguments representing the values you want to count. You can input up to 255 arguments.

  » The arguments can be individual numbers, cell references, ranges, or a combination of these. COUNT only counts numeric values. Text, empty cells, and logical values (TRUE/ FALSE) are ignored.

- **Steps to Use COUNT**:
  - » Click on the cell where you want the count.
  - » Type =COUNT(and select the range or select the cells you want to count.
  - » Press **Enter** to display the total count of numbers.

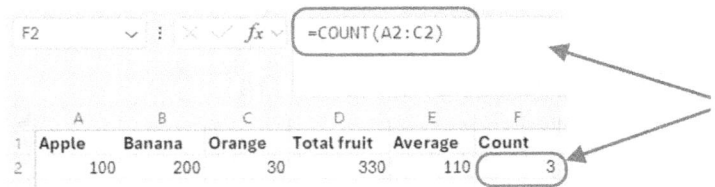

Important Note: COUNT only works with numbers. Use COUNTA to count all non-empty cells.

IV.   USING AUTOFILL

AutoFill is one of Excel's most efficient tools for quickly replicating data, creating patterns, or extending sequences in your worksheet. By mastering AutoFill, you can save time and minimize manual input when working with large datasets. This section provides a comprehensive guide to leveraging AutoFill for various scenarios.

1.   THE BASICS OF AUTOFILL

The **Fill Handle** is the small square at the bottom-right corner of a selected cell. It enables you to automatically fill adjacent cells with values, formulas, or patterns.

How to Use the Fill Handle:
  - » Select the cell(s) containing the data or formula you want to fill.
  - » Hover over the bottom-right corner of the selected cell until the cursor changes to a **plus sign (+)**.
  - » Click and drag the Fill Handle across rows or columns to fill adjacent cells. Release the mouse to complete the fill.

2.   AUTOFILL METHODS

i.   Filling the Same Data

To repeat the same value across multiple cells:
  - » Select the cell with the value.
  - » Drag the Fill Handle across the desired range.

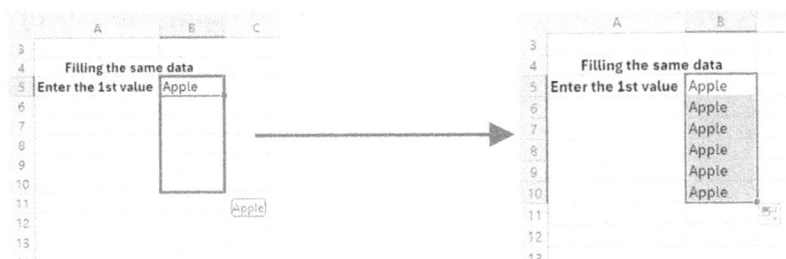

Alternatively, select all the cells (including the original), type the value in the first cell, and press Ctrl + Enter to copy the value into all selected cells.

ii. Filling Sequential Data

For sequential numbers or text patterns:

- » Enter the first few values (e.g., 1, 2).
- » Drag the Fill Handle to extend the sequence.
- » Excel will fill numbers (1, 2, 3, …) or predefined patterns (Monday, Tuesday, …).

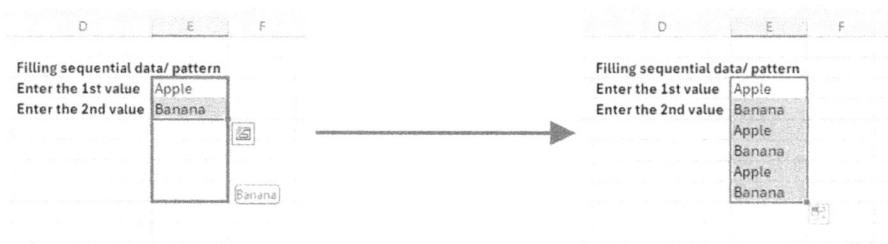

iii. Filling Non-Adjacent Cells

To fill non-adjacent cells:

- » Select multiple cells while holding **Ctrl**.
- » Enter the value in one cell and press **Ctrl + Enter**. The value will populate all selected cells.

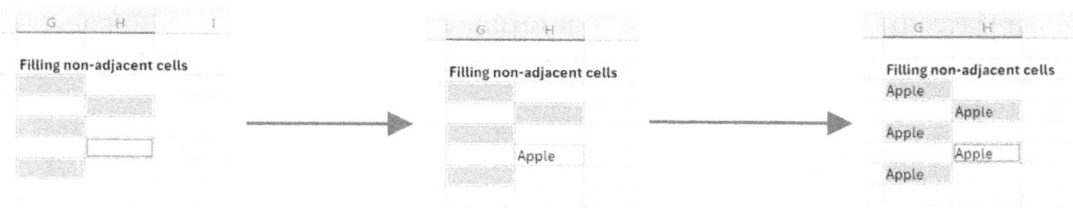

3. ADVANCED AUTOFILL SCENARIOS

i. AutoFill Dates

Excel simplifies date entry with AutoFill. The default format for dates is **MM/DD/YYYY**. Date AutoFill patterns follow your region format, so the day names or month names may differ based on system settings.

- • **Sequential Dates**: enter the first date and drag the Fill Handle to fill consecutive dates.

- **Custom Intervals**: enter two consecutive dates (e.g., 01/02/2025 and 02/02/2025), select both, and drag the Fill Handle. Excel will fill based on the interval.
- **Custom Step Values**: enter the start date, drag with the **right mouse button**, and choose **Series** from the menu. Specify the interval (e.g., every 3 days) using the **Step Value**.

ii. Filling Days, Weekdays, and Months

- **Days of the Week**:
  - » Enter the first day (e.g., Monday) and drag to auto-fill consecutive days.
  - » For custom sequences (e.g., Monday, Wednesday), enter the first two days, select them, and drag the Fill Handle.

- **Weekdays Only**:
  - » Drag the Fill Handle with the **right mouse button** and select **Fill Weekdays**.

- **Months and Years**:
  - » For months, enter the first month (e.g., January) and drag the Fill Handle.
  - » For non-sequential months or years, enter the first two values and drag.

iii. AutoFill Numbers and Series

- **Linear Series**: enter the first two numbers (e.g., 2 and 4), select them, and drag. Excel will extend the sequence (e.g., 6, 8, 10).
- **Growth Series**: enter the first two values (e.g., 2 and 4), select them, drag with the **right mouse button**, and choose **Growth Trend**.
- **Custom Series**: go to **Home > Fill > Series**, choose the type (e.g., Linear or Growth), and set the **Step Value**.

iv. AutoFill Times

- **To fill sequential times (e.g., every hour)**: enter the first time and drag the Fill Handle.

- **For non-sequential times**: enter the first two times (e.g., 8:00 AM, 9:30 AM), select them, and drag to fill based on the pattern.

4. CUSTOMIZING AUTOFILL

i. Using Custom Lists

Create custom lists for frequently used patterns:
- » Go to **File > Options > Advanced**.
- » Scroll to **General** and click **Edit Custom Lists**.
- » Enter your list (e.g., Product A, Product B) and click **Add**.

ii. AutoFill Options

After dragging the Fill Handle, click the small **AutoFill Options** icon that appears to:
- » Copy cells (repeat the value).
- » Fill series (extend a pattern).
- » Fill formatting only (apply styles without data).

5. TIPS FOR EFFICIENT USE

- **Undo Mistakes**: use **Ctrl + Z** if the AutoFill results aren't as expected.
- **Double-Click the Fill Handle**: AutoFill will extend down a column automatically if there's data in adjacent columns.
- **Explore Patterns**: experiment with numbers, text, and dates to discover patterns Excel recognizes.

AutoFill is a versatile and time-saving tool that can simplify data entry and formatting tasks. In the next section, we'll explore Flash Fill, another powerful feature for recognizing and replicating patterns in your data.

V. USING FLASH FILL

Flash Fill is a smart and intuitive tool in Excel that automatically fills data in a column based on patterns it detects from your input. It's especially useful for repetitive tasks like combining, splitting, or reformatting data without needing complex formulas. While it's simpler than AutoFill, mastering Flash Fill can significantly enhance productivity.

Flash Fill works by recognizing patterns in your data and applying them to adjacent rows. Unlike AutoFill, it doesn't require formulas or predefined series—it learns directly from examples you provide.

1. HOW TO USE FLASH FILL

1. Enter the desired result in the first cell of a new column.
2. Start typing the second result in the cell below step 1 above. Excel will display a preview of the Flash Fill results in the remaining rows.
3. Press **Enter** to accept the suggested fill or go to **Data > Flash Fill** in the ribbon.

2. COMMON USE CASES FOR FLASH FILL

i. Combining Data

Example: Merging first and last names into a full name.

» Input: Column A: John; Column B: Doe.

» Output: Column C: John Doe

» Steps: Enter "John Doe" in C1, type the second full name in C2, and apply Flash Fill.

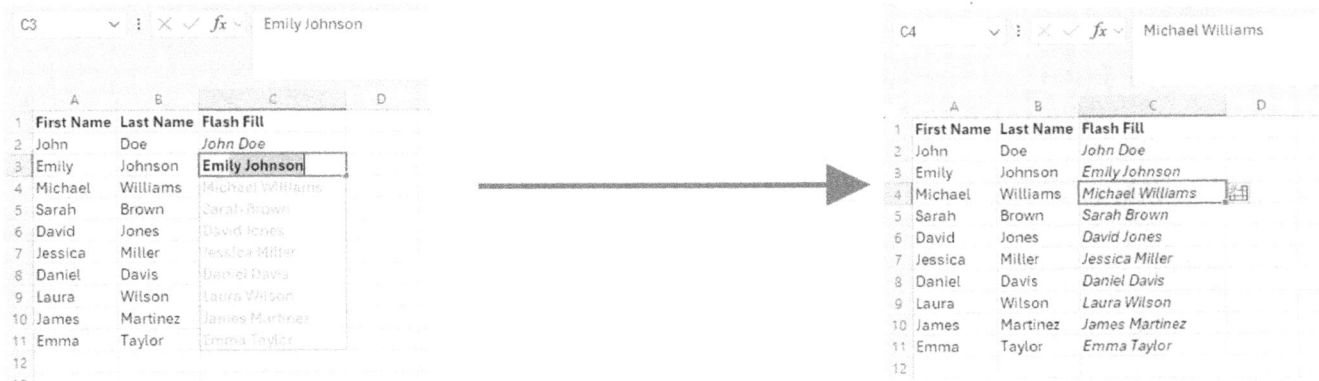

ii. Splitting Data

Example: Extracting first and last names from a full name.

» Input: Column A: John Doe

» Output: Column B: John; Column C: Doe.

» Steps: Enter "John" in B1, "Doe" in C1, and Flash Fill the rest.

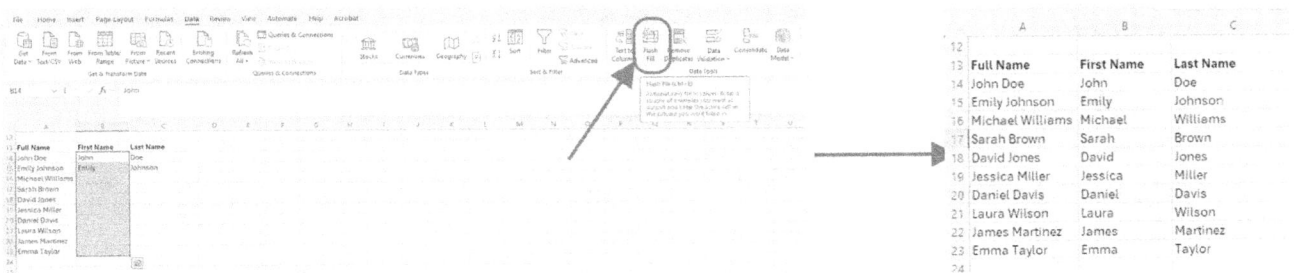

iii. Formatting Data

Example: Adding prefixes or suffixes.

» Input: Column A: 12345

» Output: Column B: ID-12345

» Steps: Enter "ID-12345" in B1, type the second formatted value, and Flash Fill.

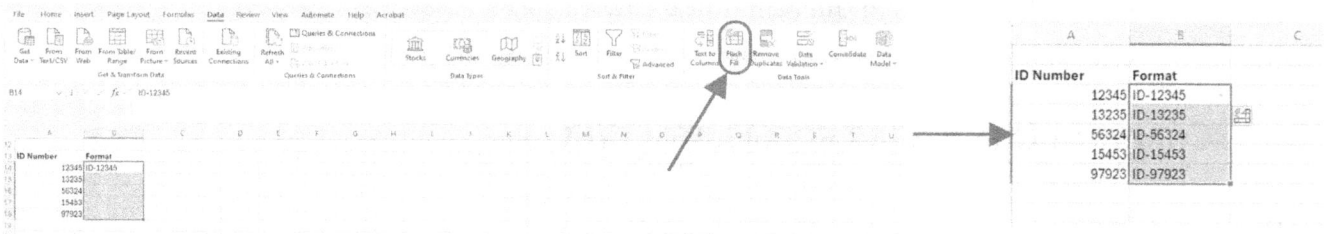

iv. Extracting Data

Example: Extracting initials from full names.

» Input: Column A: John Doe

» Output: Column B: J.D.

» Steps: Enter "J.D." in B1, type the second initials, and Flash Fill.

3. LIMITATIONS OF FLASH FILL

While Flash Fill is highly versatile, it has some limitations:

- **Consistency:** Flash Fill relies on clear and consistent patterns. If the input data is inconsistent, results may vary.

- **Manual Updates:** If the input data changes, Flash Fill doesn't update automatically like formulas.

- **Complex Logic:** For advanced tasks, using formulas or VBA might be more effective.

4. TIPS FOR EFFECTIVE USE OF FLASH FILL

- **Provide Clear Examples:** The clearer the pattern, the more accurate the results.

- **Review Output:** Always verify the Flash Fill results to ensure accuracy, especially with large datasets.

- **Enable Flash Fill:** If Flash Fill doesn't work, ensure it's enabled under File > Options > Advanced > Automatic Flash Fill.

- **Trigger Flash Fill Manually:** If Excel doesn't auto-detect the pattern, go to Data > Flash Fill or press Ctrl + E to apply Flash Fill manually.

VI. CONDITIONAL FORMATTING BASICS

Conditional formatting is a powerful feature in Excel that allows you to automatically apply formatting, such as colors, icons, or data bars, to cells based on their values or specific conditions. This tool is ideal for quickly identifying trends, highlighting outliers, or making your data visually intuitive.

Conditional formatting changes the appearance of cells in your worksheet based on the rules you define. For example:

- » Highlighting cells greater than a certain value.
- » Color-coding data to show trends or comparisons.
- » Applying data bars or icons to represent data visually.

1.   ACCESSING CONDITIONAL FORMATTING

1. Select the range of cells you want to format.
2. Go to the **Home** tab on the ribbon.
3. In the **Styles** group, click **Conditional Formatting**.
4. Choose a formatting rule from the dropdown menu.

2.   COMMON CONDITIONAL FORMATTING OPTIONS

i.   Highlight Cell Rules

These rules allow you to highlight cells that meet specific criteria.

- • **Greater Than or Less Than:**
  - » Example: Highlight all cells greater than 50.
  - » Select the range, go to **Conditional Formatting > Highlight Cell Rules > Greater Than**, enter "50," and choose a format.

- • **Equal To:**
  - » Example: Highlight all cells equal to "Pending."
  - » Select the range, go to **Conditional Formatting > Highlight Cell Rules > Equal To**, enter "Pending," and choose a format.

- **Between:**
  - » Example: Highlight cells with values between 20 and 70.
  - » Go to **Highlight Cell Rules > Between**, enter "20" and "70," and select a format.

ii. Top/Bottom Rules

Highlight cells that are at the top or bottom of a range based on value or percentage.

- **Top 10 Items:** Highlight the top 10 values in a dataset.
- **Bottom 10%:** Highlight the bottom 10% of values.

iii. Data Bars

Add colored bars inside cells to visually represent their values relative to the dataset.

- Go to Conditional Formatting > Data Bars, and select a gradient or solid bar style.

iv. Color Scales

Apply a range of colors to cells based on their values, creating a heatmap effect.

- Go to Conditional Formatting > Color Scales, and choose a preset.

v. Icon Sets

Add icons (e.g., arrows, flags, or circles) to represent data trends or categories.

- Go to Conditional Formatting > Icon Sets, and select an icon set.

3. CREATING CUSTOM RULES

For more flexibility, you can create custom formatting rules:

1. Select the range of cells.
2. Go to **Conditional Formatting > New Rule**.
3. Choose **Use a Formula to Determine Which Cells to Format**.
4. Enter a formula that defines the condition.
5. Click **Format** to select a style (e.g., color, font, or border).

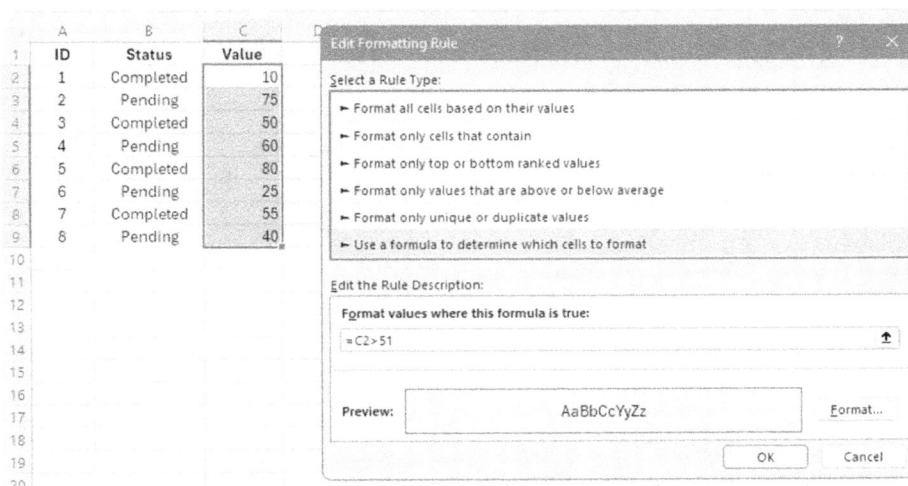

4. MANAGING CONDITIONAL FORMATTING

You can edit, clear, or prioritize conditional formatting rules:

- **Edit Rules**:
  - » Go to **Conditional Formatting > Manage Rules**.
  - » Select a rule and click **Edit Rule** to modify it.

- **Clear Rules**:
  - » To remove formatting, select the range and go to **Conditional Formatting > Clear Rules**.

- **Rule Priority**:
  - » Rules are applied in the order they appear. Use **Manage Rules** to reorder or delete conflicting rules.

VII. EXCEL TABLES

Excel tables are an essential feature that helps you organize, analyze, and visualize data more effectively. By converting a range of cells into a table, you unlock powerful tools for managing and presenting your data with ease. This section provides a detailed guide on why to use tables, their benefits, and how to create, manipulate, and filter them.

1. WHY CREATE TABLES?

Tables in Excel offer several advantages over a standard range of cells:

- **Automatic Formatting**: tables come with built-in styles, making data easier to read.
- **Dynamic Ranges**: tables expand automatically as you add or remove data.
- **Simplified Analysis**: built-in filters and sorting options allow for quick data insights.
- **Structured References**: use column names instead of cell references in formulas for clarity.
- **Improved Integration**: tables work seamlessly with charts, PivotTables, and other Excel features.

2. CREATING A TABLE

1. Select the range of data you want to convert into a table (ensure your data has headers).
2. Go to the **Insert** tab on the ribbon and click **Table**, or press **Ctrl + T**.
3. In the **Create Table** dialog box:
   » Verify the range of cells.
   » Ensure the **My Table Has Headers** checkbox is selected.
4. Click **OK**, and Excel will format the selected range as a table.

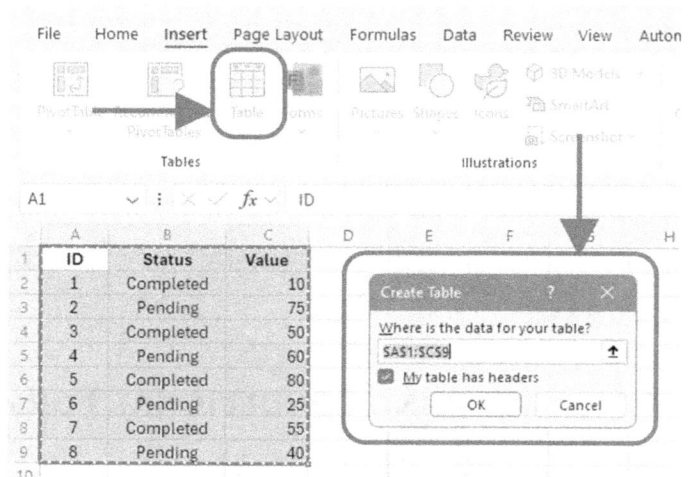

3. BENEFITS OF USING TABLES

Dynamic Data Management

- Tables automatically include new rows and columns when you add data, eliminating the need to manually adjust ranges.
- Formulas and formatting applied to a table extend dynamically to new data.

Built-In Sorting and Filtering

- Each column header includes a dropdown menu for sorting and filtering data (covered in detail below).

Total Row for Quick Calculations

- Enable the Total Row by clicking **Table Design > Total Row**. Use dropdown menus in the Total Row to quickly calculate sums, averages, counts, and more.

Enhanced Visual Appeal

- Predefined table styles and banded rows make data more readable and professional-looking.

4.   INSERTING AND REMOVING ROWS/COLUMNS IN A TABLE

i.   Inserting Rows or Columns

Adding a Row:

- Place the cursor in the last cell of the table and press **Tab** to insert a new row.
- Alternatively, right-click a row number and select **Insert > Table Rows Above**.

Adding a Column:

- Right-click a column header and select **Insert > Table Columns to the Left**.

ii.   Deleting Rows or Columns

- Right-click a row or column and select **Delete > Table Rows** or **Table Columns** to remove them.
- Be cautious when deleting data to avoid losing information unintentionally.

5.   USING FORMULAS IN TABLES

Structured References

Excel tables use **structured references**, making formulas easier to write and understand. Instead of cell references (e.g., =A1 - B1), structured references use column names (e.g., =[Sales] - [Expenses]).

D2			fx	=[@Sales]-[@Expenses]

	A	B	C	D
1	Product	Sales	Expenses	Sales - Expenses
2	1	100	80	20
3	2	200	40	160
4	3	120	50	70
5	4	160	64	96
6	5	170	73	97
7	6	180	60	120
8	7	300	180	120
9	8	80	40	40
10				

Dynamic Formula Application

When you enter a formula in one cell of a table column, Excel automatically applies it to the entire column.

Using the Total Row

- Activate the Total Row via **Table Design > Total Row**.

- Use dropdown menus in the Total Row to calculate sums, averages, counts, and other functions without writing formulas.

6. CREATING AND APPLYING TABLE STYLES

Applying Built-In Styles

- Select table and go to the **Table Design** tab.
- Choose a style from the **Table Styles** gallery to format your table instantly.

Customizing Styles

- Click **New Table Style** in the Table Styles gallery to create a custom style.
- Customize formatting for elements like headers, total rows, or banded rows/columns.

Banded Rows and Columns

- Enable **Banded Rows** or **Banded Columns** under the **Table Design** tab to alternate shading, improving readability.

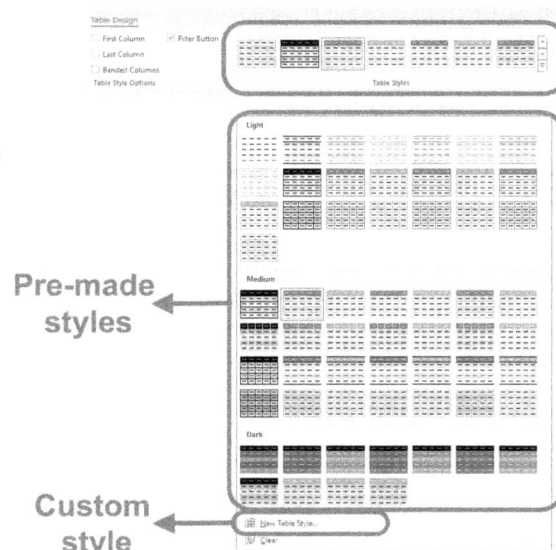

7. CONVERTING A TABLE BACK TO A RANGE

If you no longer need the table features, you can convert it back to a normal range:

- Select the table and go to the **Table Design** tab.
- Click **Convert to Range** and confirm the action. The table will retain its formatting but lose its table-specific features.

VIII. PROTECTING WORKSHEETS AND LOCKING CELLS

1. WHY PROTECT WORKSHEETS AND LOCK CELLS?

- **Prevent Accidental Changes**: Protecting your worksheet ensures that important formulas and data aren't altered unintentionally.
- **Control Data Access**: Locking cells allows you to define which parts of the worksheet users can edit.
- **Enhance Collaboration**: Enable specific permissions for collaborators to edit only designated areas.

2. LOCKING CELLS IN EXCEL

By default, all cells in Excel are locked, but this only takes effect when you protect the worksheet.

i. Steps to Lock Cells

1. Select the cells you want to lock.
2. Right-click and choose **Format Cells**, or press **Ctrl + 1** to open the **Format Cells** dialog box.
3. Navigate to the **Protection** tab.
4. Check the **Locked** option and click **OK**.

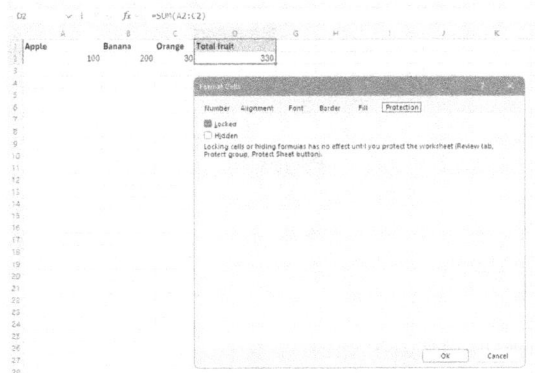

ii. Unlocking Specific Cells

If you want to allow edits to certain cells while protecting others:

1. Select the cells you want to remain editable.
2. Open the **Format Cells** dialog box.
3. Uncheck the **Locked** option and click **OK**.

3. PROTECTING A WORKSHEET

Once you've locked the desired cells, you need to protect the worksheet for the locking feature to take effect.

Steps to Protect a Worksheet

1. Go to the **Review** tab on the ribbon.
2. Click **Protect Sheet**.
3. In the **Protect Sheet** dialog box:
   » Enter a password (optional) to prevent unauthorized changes.
   » Select the actions users are allowed to perform (e.g., select unlocked cells, format cells, insert rows).
4. Click **OK** to apply protection.

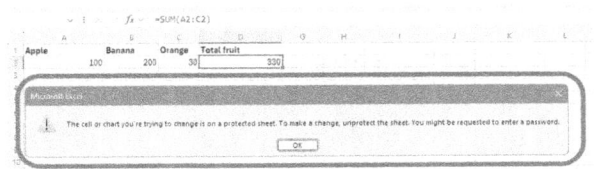

Cannot make changes

Can make changes

Password Tips

- Use a strong, memorable password.
- If you forget the password, Excel doesn't provide recovery options, so keep it safe.

4. UNPROTECTING A WORKSHEET

To unprotect a worksheet:

1. Go to the **Review** tab and click **Unprotect Sheet**.

2. Enter the password if required, and the worksheet will be unlocked.

5. ADVANCED PROTECTION OPTIONS

Protecting the Workbook

Protecting the workbook prevents structural changes like adding, deleting, or renaming sheets. Go to **Review > Protect Workbook** and choose the level of protection.

Protecting Specific Ranges

Allow different permissions for specific ranges:

1. Select the range you want to protect.
2. Go to **Review > Allow Users to Edit Ranges**.
3. Add the range, set a password (optional), and define user permissions.

File-Level Protection

Protect the entire workbook with encryption: go to **File > Info > Protect Workbook > Encrypt with Password**.

IX. PRINTING WORKSHEETS

Excel provides tools to ensure your worksheets look professional and are formatted correctly for printing.

i. Print Preview

- Before printing, go to **File > Print** to view how your worksheet will appear on paper.
- Adjust settings like margins, scaling, and page orientation from the Print Preview window.

ii. Page Setup

1. **Orientation**: choose **Portrait** (vertical) or **Landscape** (horizontal) orientation under **Page Layout > Orientation**.
2. **Margins**: adjust margins via **Page Layout > Margins** for better alignment.
3. **Scaling**: use **Fit to One Page** to scale large worksheets to fit on a single page.
4. **Headers and Footers**: add titles, dates, or page numbers via **Page Layout > Page Setup > Header/Footer**.

iii. Selecting Print Area

1. Highlight the cells you want to print.

2. Go to **Page Layout > Print Area > Set Print Area**.

3. To clear the print area, select **Clear Print Area** from the same menu.

iv. Printing Options

1. **Printing the Entire Workbook**: select **Print Entire Workbook** from the print settings.

2. **Printing Specific Sheets**: choose the sheets you want to print in the navigation pane.

3. **Printing a Selection**: highlight the desired range of cells and choose **Print Selection**.

CHAPTER 3: ESSENTIAL FORMULAS AND FUNCTIONS

I.   MATHEMATICAL FUNCTIONS (SUMIF, COUNTIF)

Mathematical functions in Excel allow you to perform calculations and analyze numeric data efficiently. Beyond basic functions like SUM and COUNT, advanced functions like **SUMIF** and **COUNTIF** provide more precise control by applying conditions to your calculations. This section explores these powerful tools and demonstrates how to use them effectively.

1.   SUMIF FUNCTION

The **SUMIF** function adds the values in a range that meet a specific condition. It is ideal for scenarios like calculating total sales for a particular region or summing expenses above a certain amount.

Syntax:
=SUMIF(range, criteria, [sum_range])

Understanding the Arguments

- **range**: this is the range of cells to evaluate against the criteria. This defines where the specified condition will be applied.
- **criteria**: this is the condition that cells must meet to be included in the sum. It can be a specific value (e.g., "Apple"), an expression (e.g., ">100"), or a cell reference (e.g., B1). The criteria must be enclosed in quotation marks if it includes symbols or text.
- **[sum_range]** (optional): This is the range containing the actual values to be summed. If omitted, Excel sums the cells in the **range** argument.

Examples of SUMIF Use Cases

- **Sales Tracking**: sum sales amounts for a specific region, a product or a certain period.
- **Expense Reports**: calculate total expenses for a specific category.
- **Gradebook Calculations**: sum scores for students scoring above 90.
- **Inventory Control**: total quantities of items in a specific category, or a certain product, or a certain zone.
- **Employee Attendance**: calculate total hours worked on a specific day.
- **Event Planning**: sum costs for specific event activities.
- **Project Management**: total hours spent on tasks assigned to a team member.

- **Customer Orders**: calculate total order amounts for a specific time period.
- **Web Analytics**: sum website visits for pages meeting specific criteria.

Tips for Using SUMIF

- **Use Wildcards**: use * to match any number of characters or ? to match a single character. For example: if you want to sum all the sales from products starting with "Apple", for the criteria, use "Apple*".
- **Relative and Absolute References**: use absolute references ($A$2:$A$20) for fixed ranges when copying formulas.
- **Error Handling**: if the range and sum_range sizes don't match, SUMIF will return an error.

Examples: We will use the dataset below for our examples.

1. **Summing Sales for product A**:
   - » Formula: =SUMIF(A1:A9,"A",B1:B9)
   - » Result: 560.

2. **Summing Expenses Above $100**:
   - » Formula: =SUMIF(C1:C9,">100") or =SUMIF(C1:C9,">100",C1:C9)
   - » Result: 415.

	A	B	C
1	Product	Sales	Expenses
2	A	100	80
3	B	200	110
4	C	120	50
5	A	160	64
6	B	170	73
7	C	180	125
8	A	300	180
9	B	80	40
10			

2. COUNTIF FUNCTION

The **COUNTIF** function counts the number of cells in a range that meet a specific condition. It's useful for counting items like the number of orders exceeding a threshold or the number of employees in a department.

Syntax:
=COUNTIF(range, criteria)

Understanding the Arguments

- **range**: This is the range of cells to evaluate against the criteria. It defines the scope of data to be analyzed.
- **criteria**: This is the condition that determines which cells to count. It can be a specific value (e.g., "Apple"), an expression (e.g., ">100"), or a cell reference (e.g., B1). The criteria must be enclosed in quotation marks if it includes symbols or text.

	A	B	C
1	Order ID	Department	Order Amount ($)
2	101	HR	450
3	102	IT	550
4	103	HR	600
5	104	Finance	300
6	105	IT	700
7	106	HR	800
8	107	Marketing	400
9	108	HR	650

Examples of COUNTIF Use Cases

- **Sales Tracking**: count the number of transactions for a specific region.
- **Inventory Management**: count items in a specific category.
- **Expense Reports**: count entries for a specific type of expense.
- **Employee Attendance**: count the number of employees who worked on a specific day.
- **Gradebook Analysis**: count students who scored above 90.
- **Project Management**: count tasks assigned to a specific team member.
- **Event Planning**: count the number of events scheduled in a specific location.
- **Customer Orders**: count the number of orders exceeding a certain amount.
- **Web Analytics**: count the number of pages with a specific keyword in their title.

Tips for Using COUNTIF

- **Use Wildcards for Flexibility**: use * to match any sequence of characters or use ? to match a single character.
- **Combine with Other Functions**: use **COUNTIF** with **SUMIF** to analyze both count and sum data for specific conditions.
- **Avoid Errors with Mismatched Data Types**: ensure the **criteria** matches the data type in the **range** (e.g., text criteria for text ranges).

Examples: We will use the dataset below for our examples.

1. **Counting Orders Over $500**:
   - » Formula: =COUNTIF(C2:C9, ">500")
   - » Result: 5.

2. **Counting Employees in the HR Department**:
   - » Formula: =COUNTIF(B2:B9, "HR")
   - » Result: 4.

Note: SUMIF and COUNTIF are not case-sensitive. 'apple' and 'Apple' are treated the same.

II.   EXTENDING TO SUMIFS AND COUNTIFS

While **SUMIF** and **COUNTIF** handle single conditions, **SUMIFS** and **COUNTIFS** allow you to apply multiple criteria, making them perfect for more complex scenarios.

1.   SUMIFS FUNCTION

The **SUMIFS** function adds values in a range that meet multiple conditions. It's an advanced version of **SUMIF** designed for scenarios involving multiple criteria.

Syntax:
=SUMIFS(sum_range, criteria_range1, criteria1, [criteria_range2, criteria2], ...)

Understanding the Arguments

- **sum_range**: The range of cells to sum.
- **criteria_range1**: The range to evaluate for the first condition.
- **criteria1**: The first condition to meet.
- Additional **criteria_range** and **criteria** pairs can be included for multiple conditions.

Examples: We will use the dataset below for our examples.

1. **Summing Sales for Region East in January**:
   » Formula: =SUMIFS(C2:C9, A2:A9, "East", B2:B9, "Jan")
   » Result: 950.

2. **Summing Expenses Greater than 200 for Region East:**
   » Formula: =SUMIFS(D2:D9, A2:A9, "East", D2:D9, ">200")
   » Result: 650.

	A	B	C	D
1	Region	Month	Sales ($)	Expenses ($)
2	East	Jan	500	150
3	East	Feb	300	200
4	West	Jan	400	300
5	East	Mar	600	250
6	West	Feb	700	100
7	North	Jan	800	300
8	East	Jan	450	400
9	South	Mar	300	150

2. COUNTIFS FUNCTION

The **COUNTIFS** function counts the number of cells that meet multiple conditions. It is an advanced version of **COUNTIF**.

Syntax:
=COUNTIFS(criteria_range1, criteria1, [criteria_range2, criteria2], ...)

Understanding the Arguments

- **criteria_range1**: The range to evaluate for the first condition.
- **criteria1**: The first condition to meet.
- Additional **criteria_range** and **criteria** pairs can be included for multiple conditions.

Examples: We will use the dataset below for our examples.

	A	B	C	D	E
1	Region	Category	Type	Month	Sales ($)
2	East	Electronics	Online	Jan	400
3	West	Clothing	In-Store	Feb	500
4	East	Electronics	In-Store	Jan	600
5	South	Grocery	Online	Mar	700
6	West	Clothing	Online	Jan	300
7	North	Grocery	In-Store	Feb	450
8	East	Electronics	Online	Jan	800
9	South	Grocery	Online	Mar	650

1. Counting Sales Transactions for a Specific Region and Month:

Task: Count the number of sales transactions in the East region during January.

» Formula: =COUNTIFS(A2:A9, "East", D2:D9, "Jan")

» Result: 3.

2. Counting Transactions by Category and Type:

Task: Count the number of Electronics transactions made Online.

» Formula: =COUNTIFS(B2:B9, "Electronics", C2:C9, "Online")

» Result: 2.

3. TIPS FOR USING SUMIFS AND COUNTIFS

Combine Multiple Conditions:

- Use logical operators (=, <, >, <>) in criteria for greater precision.
- Example: =SUMIFS(C2:C10, A2:A10, ">100", B2:B10, "<500") sums values between 100 and 500.

Use Wildcards for Flexible Matching:

- Use * for any number of characters or ? for a single character.
- Example: =COUNTIFS(A2:A10, "East*", B2:B10, "Jan*") counts entries starting with "East" in January.

Anchor Ranges:

- Use absolute references ($) for ranges when copying formulas.

Note: When using SUMIFS or COUNTIFS with dynamic arrays, you can reference spilled ranges using the # symbol (for example: A2#). Excel automatically adjusts the criteria range size.

By incorporating **SUMIFS** and **COUNTIFS**, you can handle more sophisticated data analysis tasks that require multiple conditions. These functions provide flexibility and precision, making them indispensable for complex Excel workbooks. In the next section, we'll delve into logical functions like **IF**, **AND**, **OR**, and **IFERROR**, which add decision-making capabilities to your formulas.

III. LOGICAL FUNCTIONS (IF, AND, OR, IFERROR)

Logical functions in Excel add decision-making capabilities to your formulas. They evaluate conditions and return results based on whether those conditions are true or false. This section introduces key logical functions—**IF**, **AND**, **OR**, and **IFERROR**—and their practical applications.

1. IF FUNCTION

The **IF** function allows you to perform a logical test and return different values for TRUE and FALSE outcomes. It's one of Excel's most versatile functions, enabling conditional logic in your formulas.

Syntax:
=IF(logical_test, value_if_true, value_if_false)

Understanding the Arguments

- **logical_test**: this is the condition to evaluate. It can involve comparison operators like >, <, =, or combinations with other functions.
- **value_if_true**: this is the result if the condition is TRUE. It can be a number, text, formula, or even another function.
- **value_if_false**: this is the result if the condition is FALSE. It can also be a number, text, formula, or another function.

Examples of Expanded Applications

- **Grading System**: assign letter grades based on numeric scores.
- **Business Discounts**: apply discounts based on purchase amounts.
- **Attendance Tracking**: mark employees as "Late" or "On Time" based on their arrival time.
- **Inventory Status**: highlight stock levels as "Low" or "Sufficient."
- **Expense Categorization**: classify expenses as "Over Budget" or "Within Budget."
- **Project Deadlines**: determine if tasks are overdue.
- **Dynamic Pricing**: adjust prices based on quantity purchased.

Practical Applications

- **Decision Automation**: automate decisions, e.g. determining eligibility for bonuses.
- **Conditional Formatting**: combine **IF** with conditional formatting to highlight specific data points dynamically.
- **Error Handling**: handle potential errors by combining **IF** with **ISERROR** or **IFERROR**.

Tips for Using IF

- **Simplify with Nested IFs**: avoid excessively complex nested formulas. Use newer functions like **IFS** (Excel 2016+) for clarity.
- **Combine with Logical Functions**: use **AND** or **OR** within **IF** to handle multiple conditions.
- **Avoid Hardcoding Values**: reference cells or use named ranges instead of fixed numbers or text for flexibility and reusability.

Examples: We will use the dataset below for our examples.

	A	B	C
1	Student	Score	Attendance (%)
2	John	85	90
3	Emma	65	80
4	David	50	70
5	Mia	40	95
6	Liam	95	88
7	Olivia	72	60
8	Ethan	55	75
9	Sophia	30	85

1. Simple IF Statement

Task: Determine if students passed or failed based on their score. A passing score is 60 or higher.

> » Formula: =IF(B2>=60, "Pass", "Fail")
>
> » Result:

	A	B	C	D
1	Student	Score	Attendance (%)	Result
2	John	85	90	Pass
3	Emma	65	80	Pass
4	David	50	70	Fail
5	Mia	40	95	Fail
6	Liam	95	88	Pass
7	Olivia	72	60	Pass
8	Ethan	55	75	Fail
9	Sophia	30	85	Fail

2. Nested IF Statements

Task: Assign a grade based on score: A: 85 or above; B: 70-84; C: 50-69; F: Below 50.

> » Formula: =IF(B2>=85, "A", IF(B2>=70, "B", IF(B2>=50, "C", "F")))
>
> » Result:

	A	B	C	D
1	Student	Score	Attendance (%)	Result
2	John	85	90	A
3	Emma	65	80	C
4	David	50	70	C
5	Mia	40	95	F
6	Liam	95	88	A
7	Olivia	72	60	B
8	Ethan	55	75	C
9	Sophia	30	85	F
10				

2.   AND FUNCTION

The **AND** function evaluates multiple conditions and returns TRUE only if all conditions are met. It's often used within an **IF** statement for combined logic.

Syntax:
=AND(logical1, [logical2], ...)

Understanding the Arguments

- **logical1, logical2, ...**: these are the conditions to evaluate. You can include up to 255 logical conditions in a single **AND** function. Each condition must result in either **TRUE** or **FALSE**.

Examples of Expanded Applications

- **Eligibility Check**: determine if a candidate meets multiple criteria for a loan.
- **Discount Validation**: check if a customer qualifies for a discount based on purchase quantity and total amount.
- **Inventory Restocking**: identify items that need restocking based on stock level and sales demand.
- **Project Deadlines**: check if a task is on track by evaluating completion percentage and due date.
- **Employee Attendance**: determine if an employee qualifies for a bonus based on attendance and performance rating.
- **Data Validation**: ensure entered data meets multiple criteria.

Practical Applications

- **Decision-Making**: evaluate complex conditions for business processes like approvals or eligibility.
- **Error Prevention**: validate input to ensure compliance with multiple requirements.
- **Dynamic Reporting**: highlight specific records meeting combined conditions in dashboards.

Tips for Using AND

- **Combine with IF for Decision Trees**: use **AND** inside an **IF** function to handle multiple conditions dynamically.
- **Simplify Nested Formulas**: instead of using multiple nested **IF** statements, use **AND** to simplify logic.
- **Use Cell References**: replace hardcoded values with cell references for flexibility and ease of updates.

Examples: We will use the dataset below for our examples.

1. Checking Multiple Conditions:

Task: Check if employees are eligible for promotion based on these conditions: Years of Service >= 5, and Performance Rating is "Excellent."

	A	B	C	D
1	Employee	Department	Years of Service	Performance Rating
2	John	Sales	5	Excellent
3	Emma	IT	3	Good
4	David	HR	2	Excellent
5	Mia	IT	4	Average
6	Liam	Sales	6	Good
7	Olivia	Marketing	7	Excellent
8	Ethan	IT	1	Poor
9	Sophia	HR	8	Good

» Formula: =AND(C2>=5, D2="Excellent")
» Result:

	A	B	C	D	E
1	Employee	Department	Years of Service	Performance Rating	Eligible for Promotion
2	John	Sales	5	Excellent	TRUE
3	Emma	IT	3	Good	FALSE
4	David	HR	2	Excellent	FALSE
5	Mia	IT	4	Average	FALSE
6	Liam	Sales	6	Good	FALSE
7	Olivia	Marketing	7	Excellent	TRUE
8	Ethan	IT	1	Poor	FALSE
9	Sophia	HR	8	Good	FALSE

2. Using AND with IF:

Task: Determine if employees are "Eligible" or "Not Eligible" for promotion based on the same conditions.

» Formula: =IF(AND(C2>=5,D2="Excellent"),"Eligible","Not Eligible")
» Result:

	A	B	C	D	E
1	Employee	Department	Years of Service	Performance Rating	Eligible for Promotion
2	John	Sales	5	Excellent	Eligible
3	Emma	IT	3	Good	Not Eligible
4	David	HR	2	Excellent	Not Eligible
5	Mia	IT	4	Average	Not Eligible
6	Liam	Sales	6	Good	Not Eligible
7	Olivia	Marketing	7	Excellent	Eligible
8	Ethan	IT	1	Poor	Not Eligible
9	Sophia	HR	8	Good	Not Eligible
10					

3.   OR FUNCTION

The **OR** function evaluates multiple conditions and returns TRUE if at least one condition is met. Like **AND**, it's commonly used with **IF**.

Syntax:
=OR(logical1, [logical2], ...)

Understanding the Arguments

- **logical1, logical2, ...:** these are the conditions to evaluate. You can include up to 255 conditions in a single **OR** function. Each condition must return either **TRUE** or **FALSE**.

Examples: We will use the dataset below for our examples.

	A	B	C	D
1	Student	Math Score	Science Score	Attendance (%)
2	John	85	60	92
3	Emma	45	70	88
4	David	40	35	75
5	Mia	75	80	60
6	Liam	65	50	90
7	Olivia	30	40	95
8	Ethan	90	30	85
9	Sophia	50	60	80

1.   OR Function for Award Criteria

Task: Check if students are eligible for an award based on these conditions: Math Score >= 70 or Science Score >= 70.

- » Formula: =OR(B2>=70, C2>=70)
- » Result:

	A	B	C	D	E
1	Student	Math Score	Science Score	Attendance (%)	Award Eligibility
2	John	85	60	92	TRUE
3	Emma	45	70	88	TRUE
4	David	40	35	75	FALSE
5	Mia	75	80	60	TRUE
6	Liam	65	50	90	FALSE
7	Olivia	30	40	95	FALSE
8	Ethan	90	30	85	TRUE
9	Sophia	50	60	80	FALSE

2.   Using OR with IF to Determine Eligibility

Task: Mark students as "Eligible" or "Not Eligible" based on the same criteria.

» Formula: =IF(OR(B2>=70, C2>=70), "Eligible", "Not Eligible")

» Result:

	A	B	C	D	E
1	Student	Math Score	Science Score	Attendance (%)	Award Eligibility
2	John	85	60	92	Eligible
3	Emma	45	70	88	Eligible
4	David	40	35	75	Not Eligible
5	Mia	75	80	60	Eligible
6	Liam	65	50	90	Not Eligible
7	Olivia	30	40	95	Not Eligible
8	Ethan	90	30	85	Eligible
9	Sophia	50	60	80	Not Eligible

4. IFERROR FUNCTION

The **IFERROR** function simplifies error handling by replacing error messages with custom values or text. It ensures your formulas don't break when an error occurs.

Syntax:
=IFERROR(value, value_if_error)

Understanding the Arguments

- **value**: this is the expression or formula to evaluate. This can be any calculation, such as a division, lookup, or other function.

- **value_if_error**: this is the result to return if the evaluated expression results in an error. It can be text (e.g., "Error"), a numeric value (e.g., 0), or another formula.

Common Errors Handled by IFERROR

- **#DIV/0!**: Division by zero.

- **#N/A**: Lookup functions (e.g., VLOOKUP) failing to find a match.

- **#VALUE!**: Invalid data types in formulas.

- **#REF!**: References to invalid or deleted cells.

Examples of Expanded Applications

- **Division by Zero**: handle division errors by replacing the result with a custom message.
- **Improving LOOKUPs**: avoid error messages when a value isn't found in a dataset.
- **Clean-Up Calculations**: replace errors in a dataset with default values.
- **Text Analysis**: handle errors in functions like SEARCH.
- **Dynamic Dashboards**: prevent errors from disrupting charts or summaries.
- **Data Validation**: return user-friendly messages for invalid inputs.

Examples: We will use this dataset for our example.

Task: Calculate the Sales Conversion (%) using the formula:

Sales Conversion (%) = (Sales ÷ Clicks) × 100.

Since division by zero will cause an error, use the IFERROR function to handle it gracefully.

    »   Formula: =IFERROR((C2/B2)*100, "N/A")

    »   Result:

	A	B	C
1	Campaign	Clicks	Sales
2	Campaign A	500	50
3	Campaign B	300	-
4	Campaign C	-	-
5	Campaign D	250	25
6	Campaign E	1,000	150
7	Campaign F	-	10
8	Campaign G	800	80
9	Campaign H	200	-

	A	B	C	D
1	Campaign	Clicks	Sales	Sales Conversion (%)
2	Campaign A	500	50	10
3	Campaign B	300	-	0
4	Campaign C	-	-	N/A
5	Campaign D	250	25	10
6	Campaign E	1,000	150	15
7	Campaign F	-	10	N/A
8	Campaign G	800	80	10
9	Campaign H	200	-	0

IV.   TEXT FUNCTIONS (CONCAT, TEXTJOIN, LEFT, RIGHT, MID, TRIM)

Text functions in Excel help you combine, extract, and clean text stored in your cells. These tools are useful for names, codes, addresses, ID numbers, and any text-based data you need to organize. This section introduces the essential text functions you'll use in real-world workbooks.

Excel includes both older and newer text functions. You may still encounter older formulas like CONCATENATE, but modern Excel offers improved replacements that are easier to use. All the examples here use the newer versions.

1.   COMBINING TEXT WITH CONCAT AND TEXTJOIN

i.   CONCAT Function

The CONCAT function joins two or more text strings into one. It works like the older CONCATENATE function, but it's more flexible and recommended for new formulas.

Syntax:
=CONCAT(text1, text2, …)

Understanding the Arguments

- **text1, text2, …:** The text, cell references, or numbers you want to combine.

Examples of Use Cases:

- **Combine First and Last Names**:

First Name	Last Name
John	Doe

  - » Formula: =CONCAT(A2, " ", B2)
  - » Result: "John Doe."

- **Add Prefixes or Labels**: add "ID-" before numeric IDs.
  - » Formula: =CONCAT("ID-", A2)
  - » Result: "ID-1234."

ii.   TEXTJOIN Function

TEXTJOIN is one of Excel's most useful text functions. It joins text with a delimiter (such as a space, comma, dash, or line break) and can ignore blank cells.

Syntax:
=TEXTJOIN(delimiter, ignore_empty, text1, text2, ...)

Arguments:

- delimiter: What you want between each piece of text (e.g., ", ", " ", "-")
- ignore_empty: TRUE ignores blank cells; FALSE includes them.
- text1, text2...: The text items to join.

Examples:

- Join names with a space:
  - » =TEXTJOIN(" ", TRUE, A2, B2)
  - » Result: John Doe

- Join multiple parts of an address:
  - » =TEXTJOIN(", ", TRUE, A2, B2, C2)
  - » Result: 123 Main St, Springfield, IL

Why TEXTJOIN is better: If you join several fields and some are blank, TEXTJOIN skips them automatically.

2.   EXTRACTING TEXT WITH LEFT, RIGHT, AND MID

i.   LEFT Function

LEFT extracts a certain number of characters from the start of a text string.

Syntax:
=LEFT(text, num_chars)

Examples:

- First letter of a name:
  - » =LEFT(A2, 1)
  - » Result: J
- Area code from a phone number:
  - » =LEFT(A2, 3)
  - » Result: 123

ii. RIGHT Function: RIGHT extracts characters from the end of a text string.

Syntax:
=RIGHT(text, num_chars)

Examples:

- Last 4 digits of an ID:
  - » =RIGHT(A2, 4)
  - » Result: 7890

iii. MID Function

MID extracts text from the middle of a string, starting from a specific position.

Syntax:
=MID(text, start_num, num_chars)

Example:

- If A2 contains AB-4589:
  - » =MID(A2, 4, 2)
  - » Result: 45

3. TRIM FUNCTION

TRIM removes extra spaces from text, leaving just single spaces between words. This is especially helpful when importing data from external systems.

Syntax:
=TRIM(text)

Understanding the Arguments

- **text**: The text string or cell reference to clean.

Examples of Use Cases:

- **Clean Up Imported Data**: remove unnecessary spaces from a list of names.
  » Formula: =TRIM(A1)
  » Result: "John Doe" from " John Doe ."
- **Prepare Text for Analysis**: clean data for accurate counts and comparisons.
  » Example: Convert " apple " to "apple."

Tips: You can combine with **CLEAN** to remove non-printable characters.

For example: turn "John ÆDoe" to "John Doe" by using formula =TRIM(CLEAN(A1)).

4.   MORE TEXT EXTRACTION FUNCTIONS

Excel for Microsoft 365 also includes newer functions that make text extraction easier:

- TEXTBEFORE – extracts text before a specific character
- TEXTAFTER – extracts text after a specific character
- TEXTSPLIT – splits text into columns or rows based on a delimiter

These functions reduce the need for complicated combinations of LEFT, RIGHT, MID, and FIND.

V.   DATE AND TIME FUNCTIONS

Excel stores dates and times as numbers behind the scenes, which allows you to sort them, compare them, and perform calculations such as adding days, finding deadlines, or tracking time. This section shows you the essential date and time functions you'll use in everyday spreadsheets.

1.   TODAY FUNCTION

The **TODAY** function returns the current date based on your system clock. It's dynamic, meaning it updates automatically each day.

Syntax:
=TODAY()

Examples of Use Cases:

- **Track Deadlines**: calculate days remaining until a deadline.
- **Calculate Age**: determine age based on a birthdate.
- **Dynamic Reports**: use TODAY to create daily dashboards or reports that reflect the current date.

Tips: combine with conditional formatting to highlight upcoming deadlines dynamically.

2. NOW FUNCTION

The **NOW** function returns the current date and time based on your system clock. Like **TODAY**, it updates automatically.

Syntax:
=NOW()

Examples of Use Cases:

- **Track Time-Sensitive Data**: record the time a task was completed.
  - » Formula: =NOW()
  - » Captures the exact date and time when entered.

- **Calculate Elapsed Time**: find the difference between two timestamps.
  - » Formula: =NOW() - A1
  - » Returns the elapsed time between the current moment and the timestamp in A1.

3. DATE FUNCTION

The **DATE** function creates a valid date by combining individual year, month, and day values.

Syntax:
=DATE(year, month, day)

Understanding the Arguments

- **year**: The year component of the date.
- **month**: The month component (1 for January, 12 for December).
- **day**: The day component of the date.

Examples of Use Cases:

- **Standardize Dates**: combine year, month, and day inputs into a single date.
  - » Formula: =DATE(2025, 12, 25)

» Returns: 12/25/2025.

- **Dynamic Date Calculation**: create a date for the last day of the current month.
  » Formula: =DATE(YEAR(TODAY()), MONTH(TODAY()) + 1, 0)
- **Age Calculation**: use **DATE** to calculate exact ages from a birthdate.
  » Formula: =DATEDIF(A1, DATE(YEAR(TODAY()), MONTH(A1), DAY(A1)), "y")
  » Returns the number of complete years between A1 and today.
- **Add or Subtract Days**: calculate a date 30 days from today.
  » Formula: =TODAY() + 30

4. EDATE FUNCTION

EDATE shifts a date by a specified number of months, forward or backward. This is helpful for billing cycles, subscription periods, or monthly schedules.

Syntax:
=EDATE(start_date, months)

Examples:

- Add 3 months to a date: =EDATE(A2, 3)
- Move back 1 month: =EDATE(A2, -1)
- If A2 is 1/15/2026:
  » =EDATE(A2, 3) → 4/15/2026
  » =EDATE(A2, -1) → 12/15/2025

5. EOMONTH FUNCTION

EOMONTH returns the last day of the month, shifted by a number of months. This is great for financial reports, monthly closing dates, and end-of-month reminders.

Syntax:

=EOMONTH(start_date, months)

Examples: If A2 is 1/10/2026:

- End of this month: =EOMONTH(A2, 0)
  » Result: 1/31/2026
- End of next month: =EOMONTH(A2, 1)
  » Result: 2/28/2026 (or Feb 29 in a leap year)

Notes:

- Date display is based on your system's regional format (MM/DD/YYYY or DD/MM/YYYY).
- Dates are stored as sequential numbers, so you can add or subtract days easily. Example: =A2 + 7 adds one week.
- If you see a date value as ##### (hash symbols), the column is simply too narrow — widen it to view the date.

VI. LOOKUP FUNCTIONS (VLOOKUP, XLOOKUP)

Lookup functions help you find information in a table or data range based on a value you're searching for. These formulas are useful when you need to match product codes, pull in customer details, combine lists, or search through large datasets.

The most flexible lookup function today — XLOOKUP — which replaces most older lookup formulas. However, since many existing spreadsheets still use VLOOKUP, we'll cover both so you can work confidently with both modern and legacy workbooks.

1. VLOOKUP FUNCTION (LEGACY)

The **VLOOKUP** function searches for a value in the first column of a range and returns a value in the same row from another column.

Syntax:
=VLOOKUP(lookup_value, table_array, col_index_num, [range_lookup])

Understanding the Arguments

- **lookup_value**: the value to search for in the first column of the table array. It can be a text string, number, or cell reference.
- **table_array**: the range of cells containing the data. The first column of this range is where the lookup value will be searched.
- **col_index_num**: the column number in the table array from which to return the result.
- **[range_lookup]**: this argument is optional, it specifies whether to find an exact or approximate match. Use TRUE or omit for an approximate match (table must be sorted). Use FALSE for an exact match (most common).

Examples: We will use the dataset below for our example.

	A	B	C	D
1	Product ID	Product Name	Category	Price
2	101	Widget A	Electronics	50
3	102	Widget B	Electronics	75
4	103	Widget C	Home Appliances	100
5	104	Widget D	Home Appliances	125

Task: Find the price of "Widget C" using the vertical dataset.

> » Formula: =VLOOKUP("Widget C", A2:D5, 4, FALSE)
> » Result: 100.

2.   XLOOKUP FUNCTION

The **XLOOKUP** function is a more powerful and flexible alternative to **VLOOKUP** and **HLOOKUP**. It can search both vertically and horizontally and doesn't require the lookup column to be the first column.

Syntax:
=XLOOKUP(lookup_value, lookup_array, return_array, [if_not_found], [match_mode], [search_mode])

Understanding the Arguments

- **lookup_value**: this is the value to search for in the lookup array. It can be a text string, number, or cell reference.
- **lookup_array**: the range to search for the lookup value. It can be a single column or row.
- **return_array**: this is the range to return the corresponding value from. It can be in the same row or column as the lookup array.
- **[if_not_found]**: optional; the value to return if no match is found.
- **[match_mode]**: optional; determines the type of match to perform.
  - » 0 (default): Exact match.
  - » -1: Exact match or next smaller item.
  - » 1: Exact match or next larger item.
  - » 2: Wildcard match (* for any characters, ? for a single character).
- **[search_mode]**: optional; specifies the search order.
  - » 1: Search from first to last (default).
  - » -1: Search from last to first.
  - » 2: Binary search (table must be sorted in ascending order).

Examples of Use Cases:

- **Dynamic Data Retrieval**: search for a product name and return its price.
- **Horizontal Lookup**: find sales data for a specific region.
- **Error Handling**: include a custom message when no match is found.
- **Range Lookup**: retrieve data based on approximate matches.

Examples: We will use the same dataset as VLOOKUP for our example.

Task: Find the product category for "Widget D" using the vertical dataset.

> » Formula: =XLOOKUP("Widget D", B2:B5, C2:C5)
> » Result: Home Appliances.

3.   HLOOKUP FUNCTION

HLOOKUP works like VLOOKUP, but searches across rows instead of down columns. It is rarely needed in modern Excel because XLOOKUP and INDEX/MATCH handle horizontal lookups more easily and reliably.

Syntax:
=HLOOKUP(lookup_value, table_array, row_index_num, [range_lookup])

Understanding the Arguments

- **lookup_value**: the value to search for in the first row of the table array. It can be a text string, number, or cell reference.
- **table_array**: the range of cells containing the data. The first row of this range is where the lookup value will be searched.
- **row_index_num**: the row number in the table array from which to return the result.
- **[range_lookup]**: this argument is optional; it specifies whether to find an exact or approximate match.

4.   COMPARISON OF LOOKUP FUNCTIONS

Feature	VLOOKUP	HLOOKUP	XLOOKUP
Lookup Direction	Vertical	Horizontal	Both
Requires First Column/Row	Yes	Yes	No
Multiple Search Modes	No	No	Yes
Custom Error Message	No	No	Yes

5.   TIPS FOR USING LOOKUP FUNCTIONS

- **Use XLOOKUP When Possible:** it's more versatile and eliminates the limitations of **VLOOKUP** and **HLOOKUP**.
- **Sort Data for Approximate Matches:** ensure the lookup array is sorted in ascending order when using approximate match (TRUE or 1).
- **Error Handling:** for older versions of Excel, pair **VLOOKUP** or **HLOOKUP** with **IFERROR** for cleaner outputs.

VII. A QUICK PREVIEW OF DYNAMIC ARRAY FUNCTIONS

Excel includes a set of powerful formulas called dynamic array functions. These formulas can return multiple results at once, and Excel automatically "spills" those results into neighboring cells. This means you don't need to copy formulas down or across, Excel generates all the output for you.

You don't need to master these functions yet. You'll learn them in detail in later chapters, but here's a quick look so you understand what's coming.

1. WHAT IS A DYNAMIC ARRAY?

When a formula returns more than one value, Excel places the extra results into the cells below or beside the formula. This is called a spill range.
For example, if a formula produces five results, Excel fills five cells automatically.

If you reference a spilled range in another formula, use the # symbol: =SUM(C2#)
This tells Excel to use the entire spilled range created by the formula in C2.

2. WHY DYNAMIC ARRAYS MATTER

Dynamic array formulas are easier to build, easier to read, easier to update and more flexible than older formulas. They also work beautifully with Tables, XLOOKUP, data cleanup steps, dashboard formulas and pivot table preparation.

You'll start using these dynamic array functions in later chapters, especially when we work with data cleaning and advanced formulas.

3. KEY DYNAMIC ARRAY FUNCTIONS

- SORT: Sorts a range of data automatically.
  =SORT(A2:A10)
- FILTER: Extracts rows that match a condition.
  =FILTER(A2:C10, C2:C10="North")
- UNIQUE: Returns a list of unique items.
  =UNIQUE(A2:A20)
- SEQUENCE: Creates a list of numbers without typing them manually.
  =SEQUENCE(10)
  » Creates numbers 1 through 10.

If Excel shows a #SPILL! error, something is blocking the cells where the results need to appear. Just clear the cells around the formula and try again.

CHAPTER 4: WORKING WITH DATA

I.   SORTING AND FILTERING DATA

Sorting and filtering data in Excel are essential tools for organizing and analyzing large datasets. They help you quickly locate information, rank values, and focus on specific subsets of data.

1.   SORTING DATA

Sorting allows you to arrange data in a specific order, either ascending or descending, based on one or more columns.

i.   Types of Sorting:

- **Single-Column Sorting**: sort a single column in ascending or descending order.
- **Multi-Level Sorting**: sort by one column and then by another for hierarchical organization.

ii.   Steps to Sort Data:

Sort a Single Column:

1. Select the column to sort.
2. Go to the **Data** tab and click **Sort A to Z** (ascending) or **Sort Z to A** (descending).

Sort by Multiple Columns:

3. Select the data range (including headers).
4. Click **Sort** under the **Data** tab.
5. In the **Sort** dialog box: choose the first column to sort by, and add additional levels to sort by secondary criteria.

Example:

- » **Task:** sort above data by department, then by years of service.

	A	B	C
1	Employee Name	Department	Years of Service
2	John Smith	IT	5
3	Emma Johnson	HR	3
4	David Brown	IT	2
5	Mia Davis	Sales	4
6	Liam Wilson	IT	5
7	Olivia Miller	HR	6

» **Steps:**

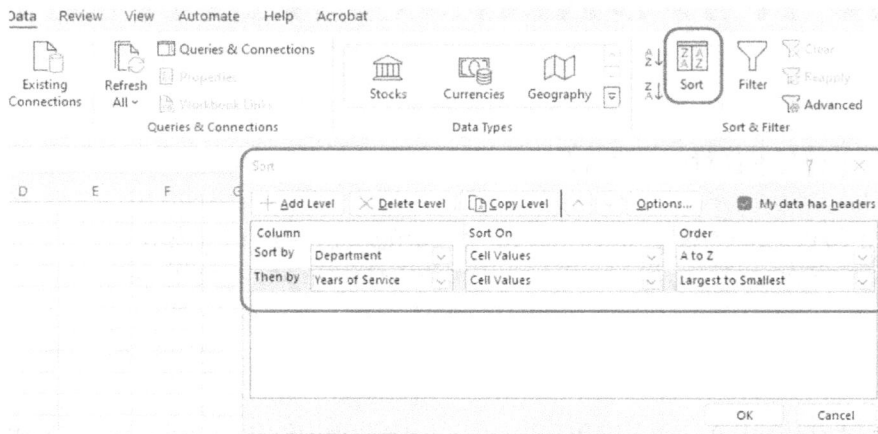

» **Result:**

	A	B	C
1	Employee Name	Department	Years of Service
2	Olivia Miller	HR	6
3	Emma Johnson	HR	3
4	John Smith	IT	5
5	Liam Wilson	IT	5
6	David Brown	IT	2
7	Mia Davis	Sales	4

iii. Practical Use Cases:

- **Sales Data**: Rank products by sales volume.
- **Attendance Records**: Arrange employees alphabetically.

2. FILTERING DATA

Filtering helps you display only the rows that meet specific criteria while hiding the rest. It's a powerful tool for focusing on relevant data in large datasets.

i. Types of Filters:

- **Text Filters**: filter text-based columns by specific values, partial matches, or custom conditions.
- **Number Filters**: filter numeric data using conditions like greater than, less than, or between.
- **Date Filters**: filter date-based columns by time periods, such as today, last month, or custom ranges.

ii. Steps to Apply Filters:

1. Select the data range or place the cursor in the dataset.
2. Go to the **Data** tab and click **Filter**.
3. Dropdown arrows appear in the header row.
4. Use the dropdown menu to apply filters:
   - » For text columns, choose specific values or use options like **Contains** or **Does Not Contain**.
   - » For numeric columns, use options like **Greater Than** or **Less Than**.
   - » For date columns, select ranges like **Last Week** or **Next Month**.

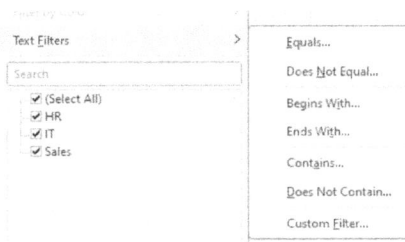

3. CUSTOM SORT AND FILTER OPTIONS

Custom Lists for Sorting: define a custom order (e.g., sort days as Monday, Tuesday, Wednesday).

   - » Go to **File > Options > Advanced > General > Edit Custom Lists**.

Advanced Filter: use complex criteria for filtering.

   - » Go to **Data > Advanced** and define a criteria range.

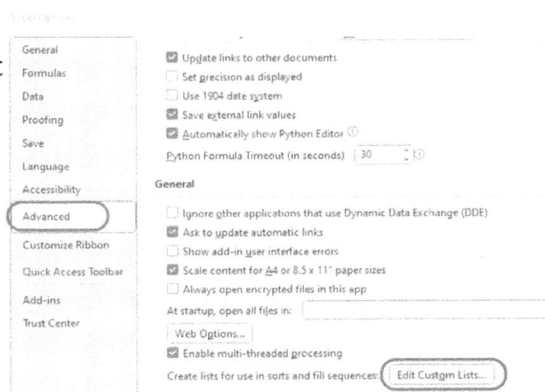

II. DATA VALIDATION: DROPDOWN LISTS AND RULES

1. WHAT IS DATA VALIDATION?

Data validation is a feature that restricts the type, range, or format of data that can be entered into cells. It can be used to define specific criteria for valid inputs, create dropdown menus for selecting predefined options or display warnings or messages when invalid data is entered.

2. CREATING DROPDOWN LISTS

Dropdown lists simplify data entry by allowing users to select from a predefined set of values.

i. Steps to Create a Dropdown List

1. **Prepare the List**:
   - » Enter the list of valid values in a separate range (e.g., A2:A8).
2. **Apply Data Validation**:
   - » Select the cell or range where the dropdown will appear.
   - » Go to the **Data** tab and click **Data Validation**.
   - » In the **Data Validation** dialog box: set **Allow** to **List**.

» Set the **Source** to the range containing your list (A2:A8).

3. **Optional Enhancements**:

    » **Error Alert**: Display a warning if invalid data is entered.

    » **Input Message**: Add a tooltip to guide users.

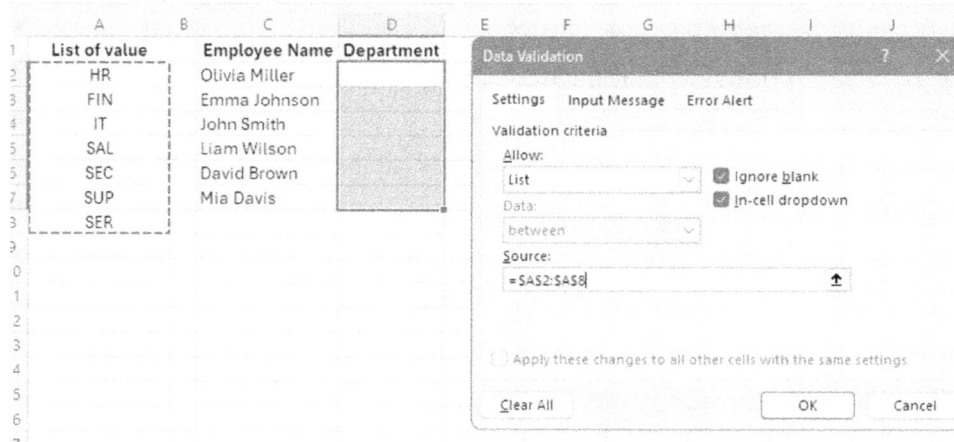

ii. Practical Use Cases:

*   **Order Forms**: Allow users to select product names from a dropdown.
*   **Project Management**: Create status dropdowns with options like "In Progress," "Completed," and "Pending."

3. DEFINING VALIDATION RULES

Validation rules restrict data based on numeric, text, date, or custom criteria.

Common Validation Rules:

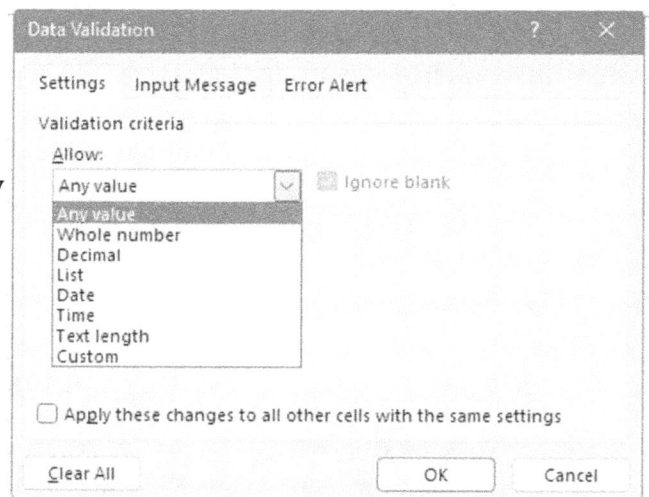

1. **Whole Numbers**: restrict inputs to integers within a range.

    » Set **Allow** to **Whole Number** and specify the **Minimum** and **Maximum** values.

2. **Decimal Numbers**: allow decimal values within a specific range.

3. **Dates**: restrict inputs to specific date ranges.

    » Set **Allow** to **Date** and define the start and end dates.

4. **Text Length**: limit the number of characters.

5. **Custom Formulas**: use formulas for complex rules.

4.   HANDLING INVALID DATA

When invalid data is entered, Excel can display:

- **Stop Message**: Prevents entry and shows an error message.
- **Warning Message**: Warns the user but allows invalid entry.
- **Information Message**: Notifies the user but permits the entry.

Steps to Configure Error Alerts:

1.   In the **Data Validation** dialog box, go to the **Error Alert** tab.
2.   Choose the style (Stop, Warning, or Information).
3.   Enter a custom title and message for the alert.

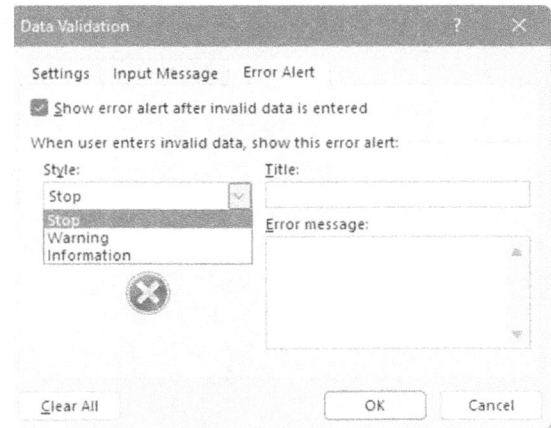

5.   EDITING AND REMOVING VALIDATION

Edit Validation Rules:

» Select the cell or range with validation.

» Go to **Data > Data Validation** and modify the criteria.

Remove Validation:

» Select the cells.

» Open the **Data Validation** dialog box and click **Clear All**.

6.   USING LAMBDA IN DATA VALIDATION

i.   Introducing the LAMBDA Function

The LAMBDA function lets you create your own custom functions in Excel. A LAMBDA function takes inputs, performs a calculation, and returns a result. Once created, you can reuse it throughout your workbook just by calling its name, which makes your formulas cleaner and easier to maintain.

Syntax:
=LAMBDA(parameter1, parameter2, ..., calculation)

- Parameters are placeholder names you assign (like x, y, range).
- Calculation is the formula Excel should run using those parameters.

You can store a LAMBDA function in the Name Manager so it behaves like a normal Excel function.

Key features:

- Create reusable custom functions without VBA.

- Simplify long or repeated formulas.

- Combine with newer functions like IF, FILTER or REGEXTEST (see page .

- Make data validation and cleaning rules more powerful.

- Share logic across multiple sheets consistently.

LAMBDA is an advanced feature, but once you learn it, it lets you build your own toolkit of custom Excel functions tailored to your work.

ii.   Using LAMBDA in Data Validation

Example: you need to send a template to HR department to fill in all employees' names. You'll create a named LAMBDA function called LettersOnly, then use it in Data Validation so a column only accepts A–Z letters (no numbers or symbols).

Create the LAMBDA function

1.   Go to the Formulas tab. Click Name Manager (or Define Name), then click New....

2.   In Name, type: LettersOnly.

3.   In Refers to, type this formula: =LAMBDA(x, REGEXTEST(x, "^[A-Za-z]+$"))

4.   Select the range where names go, for example: A2:A100 (start at the first data row).

5.   Go to Data → Data Validation. On the Setting tab, set Allow to Custom, then set Formula to =IFERROR(LettersOnly(A2)=TRUE, FALSE).

6.   On the Error Alert tab: select "Show error alert after invalid data is entered", select Style as Stop and input Error Message. Then click OK.

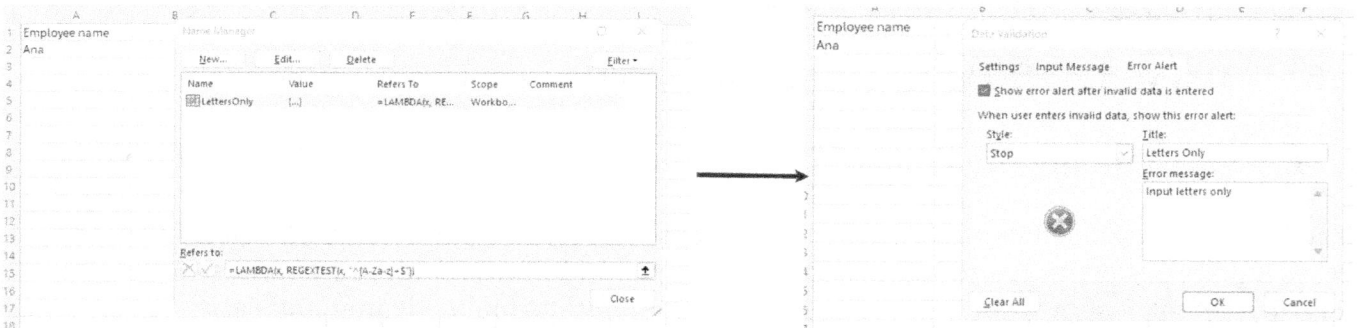

Result:

When users type in characters that are not letters, it will trigger the error message.

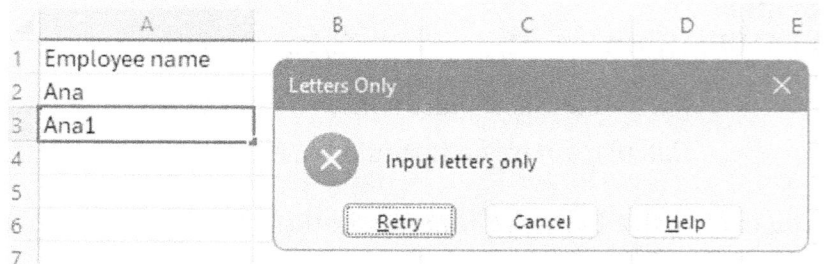

7. PRACTICAL TIPS FOR DATA VALIDATION

Dynamic Dropdown Lists: use a named range or **OFFSET** formula to create dynamic lists that update automatically when new items are added.

Combining with Conditional Formatting: highlight invalid entries by applying conditional formatting to cells that don't meet the validation rules.

Use Custom Messages for Clarity: guide users by adding input messages that explain the criteria.

III. CLEANING DATA USING FIND & REPLACE, AND REMOVE DUPLICATES

1. CLEANING DATA WITH FIND & REPLACE

The **Find & Replace** tool allows you to locate specific values in your dataset and replace them with new values. It's versatile and can handle a wide range of data-cleaning tasks.

i. Steps to Use Find & Replace:

1. **Access the Tool**:
   » Go to **Home > Find & Select > Replace** or press Ctrl + H.

2. **Find Specific Values**:
   » In the **Find what** box, enter the value to search for.
   » In the **Replace with** box, enter the replacement value.

3. **Replace Options**:
   » Click **Replace All** to update all instances in the worksheet.
   » Click **Replace** to update one instance at a time.

ii. Common Use Cases:

- **Standardizing Text**: replace inconsistent text entries (e.g., "NYC" with "New York").
- **Correcting Errors**: fix typos or formatting errors in large datasets (e.g., find "janury", replace with "January").
- **Cleaning Special Characters**: remove unwanted characters like underscores (_) or hashtags (#).
- **Updating Data**: replace outdated information with current data.

2. CLEANING DATA WITH REMOVE DUPLICATES

Duplicate values can skew your analysis and result in inaccurate insights. The **Remove Duplicates** tool eliminates these redundancies efficiently.

i. Steps to Remove Duplicates:

1. Select the Data:

» Highlight the range of data to clean.

2. Access the Tool:

» Go to **Data > Remove Duplicates**.

3. Configure Columns:

» In the dialog box, select the columns to check for duplicates.

» Deselect columns that should not affect the duplication criteria.

4. Remove Duplicates:

» Click **OK** to remove duplicates. Excel will display a summary of duplicates removed and unique values retained.

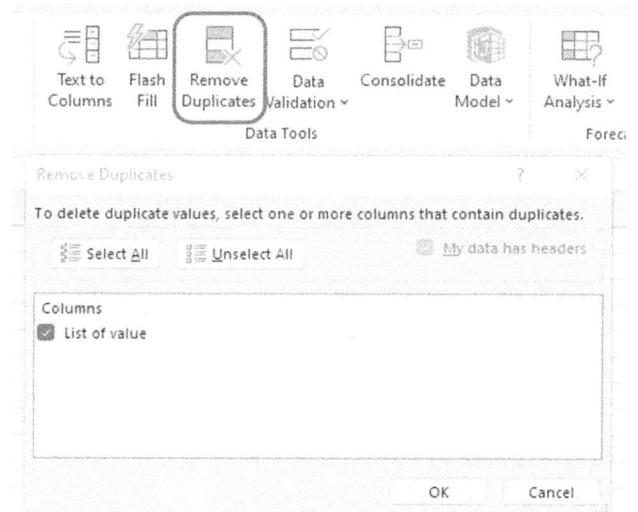

ii. Common Use Cases:

- **Cleaning Customer Data**: eliminate duplicate customer entries based on names, emails, or phone numbers. Example: Remove duplicates from a "Customer ID" column.

- **Inventory Management**: identify unique products by SKU or item name. Example: Remove duplicates from a "Product SKU" column.

- **Survey Responses**: ensure only unique responses are retained for analysis. Example: Remove duplicates from an "Email" column in a survey dataset.

3. COMBINING FIND & REPLACE WITH REMOVE DUPLICATES

These tools can be used together for comprehensive data cleaning:

- **Standardize Data**: use **Find & Replace** to correct inconsistencies, then remove duplicates to ensure unique entries.

- **Fix Formatting**: replace special characters or extra spaces, then remove duplicate values caused by minor variations.

IV. SPLITTING DATA (TEXT TO COLUMNS)

Splitting data is key operations for cleaning and organizing information in Excel. Splitting data allows you to separate text into multiple columns. The **Text to Columns** tool is particularly useful for splitting data efficiently.

The **Text to Columns** tool splits data in a single column into multiple columns based on a delimiter or fixed width.

1. STEPS TO USE TEXT TO COLUMNS:

1. **Select the Data**:
   » Highlight the column containing the data you want to split.

2. **Access the Tool**:
   » Go to **Data > Text to Columns**.

3. **Choose the Data Type**:
   » Select **Delimited** if the data is separated by specific characters (e.g., commas, spaces).
   » Select **Fixed Width** if the data is split at specific character positions.

4. **Configure Delimiters or Widths**:
   » For **Delimited**, choose the delimiter (e.g., comma, tab, space).
   » For **Fixed Width**, set break lines to indicate column divisions.

5. **Select Destination**:
   » Choose where the split data will appear. The default is to overwrite the original column.

6. **Complete the Process**:
   » Click **Finish** to split the data.

Example: split below dataset to 2 columns for first name and last name.

Employee Name
Olivia Miller
Emma Johnson
John Smith
Liam Wilson
David Brown
Mia Davis

   » Steps:

» Result:

Employee Name	
Olivia	Miller
Emma	Johnson
John	Smith
Liam	Wilson
David	Brown
Mia	Davis

2. USING POWER QUERY TO SPLIT COLUMNS

Text to Columns is perfect for quick, one-time splits. However, if you need to repeat the same split on new data or handle more complex patterns, Power Query is a better choice. Power Query lets you define the split once and then refresh it whenever the data changes.

1. Loading Data into Power Query
   » Select any cell inside your data range. Go to the Data tab.
   » In the Get & Transform Data group, click From Table/Range.
   » Check the range and tick My table has headers if your data includes headers. Click OK.
   » Excel opens the Power Query Editor with your data.

2. Select the column you want to split
   » Click the header of the column that contains the text you want to split.
   » On the Ribbon, go to Home → Split Column (or Transform → Split Column). Pick the method: delimiter, number, positions, etc.
   » Configure the split according to your split method.

3. Rename the new columns
   » Power Query will create new column names (such as Column1.1, Column1.2).
   » Double-click the headers and rename them to something meaningful.

4. Load the results back to Excel
   » Go to Home → Close & Load.
   » Excel creates a new table with the split columns.
   » When the original data changes, use Data → Refresh to reapply all steps automatically.

Example:

Split the Department Code below into 2 columns: Department and Number.

	A
1	**Code**
2	IT-001
3	MKT-015
4	HR-105
5	LEG-220
5	FIN-320

Step-by-step instruction:

1. Select a cell in the data and go to Data → From Table/Range, then click OK.
2. In Power Query, click the Code column header.
3. Go to Home → Split Column → By Delimiter...
4. In Delimiter, choose Custom and type a dash: -.
5. Under Split at, keep Each occurrence of the delimiter.
6. Under Advanced options, keep Split into Columns selected and click OK.
7. Rename the new columns: First column → Department, Second column → Number
8. Click Home → Close & Load.

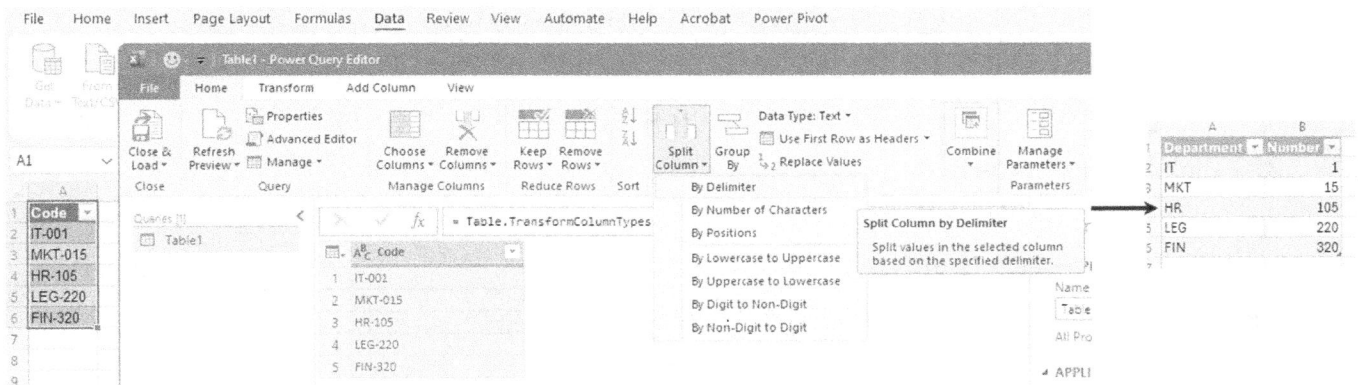

3. PRACTICAL APPLICATIONS

- **Data Preparation for Import:** split concatenated fields (e.g., "Name: John" to "Name" and "John") for easier processing.

- **Report Customization:** Break down summary data (e.g., "Region:Sales" into "Region" and "Sales") for enhanced report visualization.

- **Sales Analysis:** Divide customer information, product details, or transaction data into meaningful segments for insights.

V. USING REGEX FUNCTIONS TO CLEAN AND EXTRACT TEXT

Modern Excel includes three REGEX functions that make it easier to clean data, validate text, extract certain patterns, and standardize formatting. These functions are especially useful when working with product codes, IDs, dates, messy imports, or any text that follows a predictable structure.

1. THE THREE REGEX FUNCTIONS IN EXCEL

Excel provides three REGEX functions:

- **REGEXTEST** – checks if text matches a pattern (returns TRUE/FALSE).
- **REGEXEXTRACT** – extracts text that matches a pattern.
- **REGEXREPLACE** – replaces matching text with something else.

You don't need to memorize regex rules — you only need a few simple patterns to clean most real-world data.

2. STEPS FOR USING REGEX FUNCTIONS

Use these steps anytime you want to clean, validate, or extract text based on a pattern.

1. Identify the text you want to fix or extract
   » Common examples: product codes, employee IDs, phone numbers, email domains, numbers inside text.

2. Choose the right regex function
   » Use REGEXTEST when you want Excel to answer yes/no.
   » Use REGEXEXTRACT when you want Excel to pull out part of the text.
   » Use REGEXREPLACE when you want to remove or fix certain characters.

3. Pick a regex pattern
   » \d+ → any digits
   » [A-Za-z]+ → letters only
   » [^A-Za-z0-9] → anything that is not a letter or number
   » @(.+)$ → everything after the @ symbol
   » ^\d{3} → first three digits

4. Write the formula in the next column
   » Enter the REGEX formula (examples below).
   » Fill it down as needed.

5. (Optional) Convert results to values
   » If you want to replace your original data, copy the results and choose Paste → Values.

3. EXAMPLE FOR USING REGREX

Suppose you have a dataset as below and you need to extract the numeric part only. The dataset is inconsistent in terms of formatting.

Item
A-5001 : Available
B-223 :   Not Available
C-9999: Low

Instruction:

1. In an empty column, enter this formula: =REGEXEXTRACT(A2, "\d+")
2. Fill the formula down the column. You will receive the numeric part only

4.   WHEN TO USE REGEX INSTEAD OF STANDARD TEXT FUNCTIONS

Regex functions are especially helpful when:

- The pattern varies in length
- You need to extract text buried inside messy strings
- You want to clean imported data quickly
- Standard functions (LEFT, RIGHT, MID) would require many nested formulas

If your data has structure, even if the structure is messy, regex can usually extract or clean it in one formula.

VI.   USING COPILOT

Excel includes two AI helpers: Copilot Chat and the full Microsoft 365 Copilot version.

- Copilot Chat is already rolling out to most Microsoft 365 users. You can open it from the ribbon and ask questions, get help writing formulas, and learn steps without a separate subscription.
- Microsoft 365 Copilot is the paid add-on that unlocks full editing and automation features (such as sorting, filtering, cleaning, modifying workbook content) inside Excel and other apps. A subscription is required.

If you don't have the full version, you can still use Copilot Chat to support your work — you'll just perform the actions yourself instead of having AI apply them automatically.

Examples you can use:

- "Sort this table by Department, then by Years of Service."
- "Filter to show only rows where Sales are greater than 10,000."
- "Show only the people in the Marketing department."
- "Clear all filters."

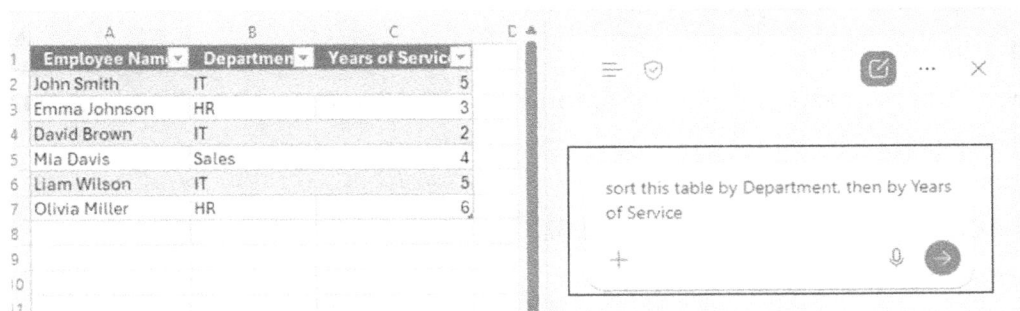

Copilot will apply the steps or guide you through them. This is especially helpful when working with large datasets.

CHAPTER 5: DATA VISUALIZATION

I. CREATING BASIC CHARTS: BAR, LINE, AND PIE CHARTS

Charts are powerful tools for visualizing data and gaining insights. In this section, we'll explore the most commonly used charts — bar, line, and pie charts — including their use cases, examples, steps to create them, and additional tips for effective visualization.

1. BAR CHARTS

Use Cases: bar charts are ideal for comparing data across categories.

- **Sales Analysis**: Compare revenue across different regions.
- **Project Management**: Visualize tasks completed by team members.
- **Survey Results**: Display responses by category.

Steps to Create a Bar Chart:

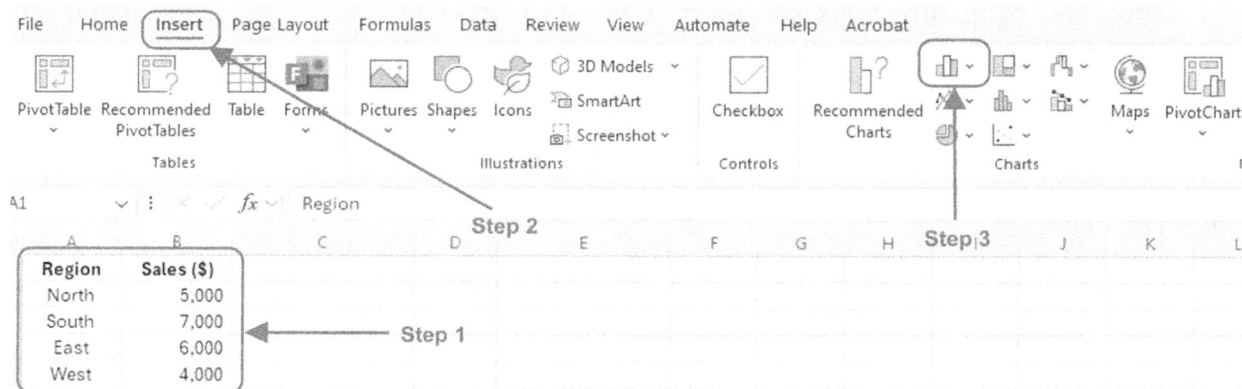

1. Select the data range (e.g., A1:B5).
2. Go to the **Insert** tab.
3. In the **Charts** group, click **Insert Column or Bar Chart** and choose a bar chart type.
4. Customize the chart using the **Chart Tools** ribbon:
    » Add axis titles, labels, and a chart title;
    » Format bars with custom colors.

Example result:

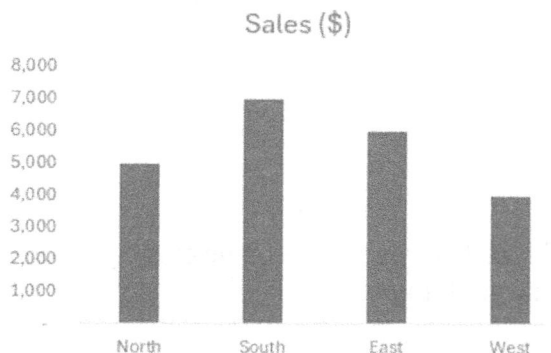

Notes:

- Use horizontal bars for clearer comparisons when category names are long.
- Combine with a secondary axis if needed for multi-variable comparisons.

2. LINE CHARTS

Use Cases: line charts are excellent for showing trends over time.

- **Sales Growth**: Track revenue over months or years.
- **Website Analytics**: Visualize traffic trends.
- **Temperature Data**: Show daily temperature changes.

Steps to Create a Line Chart:

1. Select the data range (e.g., A1:B5).
2. Go to the **Insert** tab.
3. In the **Charts** group, click **Insert Line or Area Chart** and select a line chart.
4. Customize the chart by:
   » Adding a title, data labels, and gridlines.
   » Formatting the line style and color.

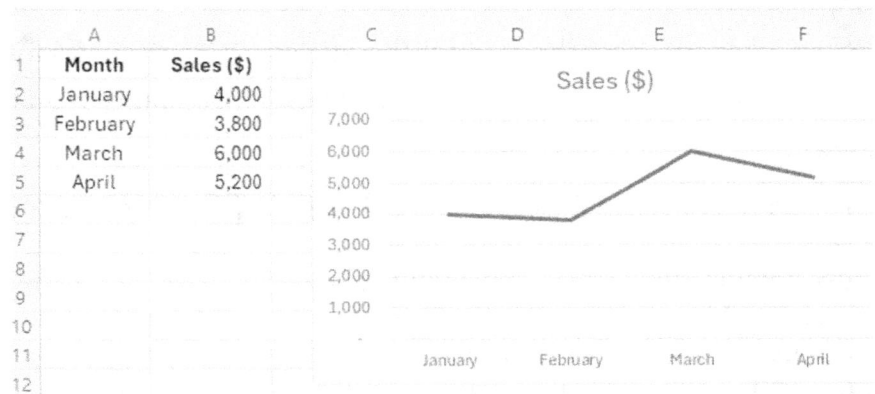

	Month	Sales ($)
1	Month	Sales ($)
2	January	4,000
3	February	3,800
4	March	6,000
5	April	5,200

Other Notes:

- Use markers on the line to highlight specific data points.

3. PIE CHARTS

Use Cases: pie charts are great for showing proportions or parts of a whole.

- **Budget Allocation**: Display spending by category.
- **Market Share**: Show the distribution of market share among competitors.
- **Survey Analysis**: Visualize response percentages.

Steps to Create a Pie Chart:

1. Select the data range (e.g., A1:B5).
2. Go to the **Insert** tab.
3. In the **Charts** group, click **Insert Pie or Doughnut Chart** and choose a pie chart.

4. Customize the chart by:

  » Adding data labels to show percentages.

  » Pulling out slices to emphasize specific categories (exploded pie chart).

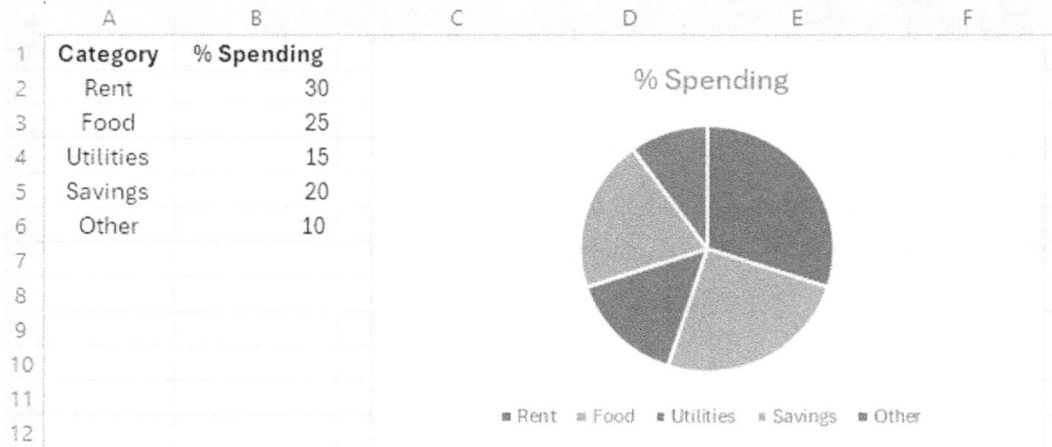

Notes:

- Avoid using too many slices; stick to 5–7 categories for clarity.
- Combine with legends or data labels to enhance readability.

II. CUSTOMIZING CHART STYLES AND LAYOUTS

Customizing chart styles and layouts allows you to enhance the visual appeal and clarity of your charts, making them more effective for communicating insights. Excel offers various customization options to ensure your charts align with your data story.

1. WHY CUSTOMIZE CHARTS?

Improve Readability: Highlight key data points and make the chart easier to interpret.

Enhance Visual Appeal: Use colors, fonts, and layouts to make charts more engaging.

Focus Attention: Draw attention to critical insights with annotations or specific styles.

2. KEY CUSTOMIZATION OPTIONS

i. Chart Styles

Excel provides predefined chart styles that you can apply to your charts for a professional look.

Steps to Apply a Chart Style:

1. Click on the chart to activate it.
2. Go to the **Chart Tools > Design** tab.
3. In the **Chart Styles** group, hover over a style to preview it and click to apply.

ii.　Chart Layouts

Chart layouts define the arrangement of elements like titles, legends, and labels.

Steps to Change Chart Layout:

1. Select the chart.
2. Go to the **Chart Tools > Design** tab.
3. In the **Chart Layouts** group, choose a predefined layout or customize manually.

iii.　Manual Customization Options:

Add or Edit Chart Titles:

»　Go to **Chart Tools > Layout > Chart Title**.

»　Select **Above Chart** or **Centered Overlay Title**.

»　Click on the title to edit the text.

Add Data Labels:

»　Select the chart and go to **Chart Tools > Layout > Data Labels**.

»　Choose from options like **Center**, **Inside End**, or **Outside End** to display values on the chart.

Modify Legend Position:

»　Go to **Chart Tools > Layout > Legend**.

»　Move the legend to the **Top**, **Right**, **Left**, or **Bottom**, or hide it if unnecessary.

Gridlines:

»　Enable or disable gridlines to simplify the chart view.

»　Go to **Chart Tools > Layout > Gridlines** and select **Primary Major Gridlines** or **Primary Minor Gridlines**.

Axis Customization:

»　Format the axis to display data more effectively.

»　Right-click the axis and choose **Format Axis** to adjust scaling, intervals, or display options.

3. FORMATTING CHARTS

Beyond styles and layouts, Excel allows granular formatting to enhance chart appearance.

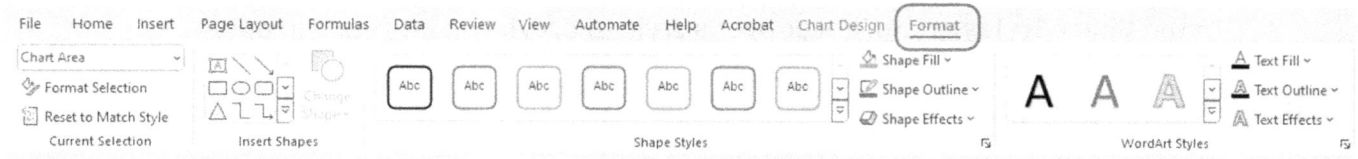

Change Chart Colors:

  » Select the chart.

  » Go to **Chart Tools > Format > Shape Fill** or **Shape Outline**.

  » Choose custom colors to match your theme or emphasize specific data.

Use Custom Fonts:

  » Click on any chart text element (title, labels, or legend).

  » Go to the Home tab and select a font style, size, or color.

Apply Effects:

  » Select the chart element to apply effects.

  » Go to **Chart Tools > Format > Shape Effects**.

  » Add shadows, glow, or 3D effects to enhance the visual appeal.

4. USE CASES

Highlighting Trends in a Line Chart:

  » Add data labels to peaks and troughs to emphasize trends.

  » Use a contrasting color for the trendline.

Customizing a Bar Chart for Sales Data:

  » Apply a gradient fill to bars to differentiate regions.

  » Place the legend at the top for better visibility.

Polishing a Pie Chart for Budget Proportions:

  » Add percentage labels for each slice.

  » Use an exploded pie chart to highlight key categories.

5. EXAMPLE: CUSTOMIZING A BAR CHART FOR REGIONAL SALES

We will use below dataset for our example:

	A	B
1	Region	Sales ($)
2	North	5,000
3	South	7,000
4	East	6,000
5	West	4,000

Steps to Create the Chart:

>> Highlight the data range (A1:B5).

>> Go to **Insert > Bar Chart > Clustered Bar.**

>> A bar chart appears with default styling.

Customization tasks:

>> **Add a Chart Title**: Replace the default title with "Regional Sales."

>> **Change Bar Colors**: Select bars and apply a gradient from blue to green.

>> **Move the Legend**: Place the legend at the top for better visibility.

>> **Display Data Labels**: Add labels to show exact sales figures on each bar.

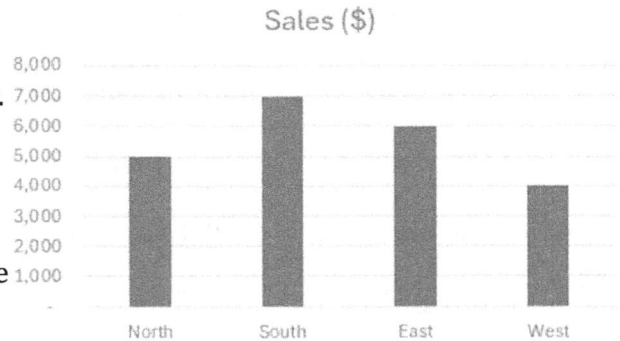

Result:

III.   USING SPARKLINES FOR QUICK INSIGHTS

Sparklines are mini-charts embedded within a single cell in Excel. They provide a quick and compact way to visualize trends and patterns in your data without taking up much space.

1.   WHAT ARE SPARKLINES?

Sparklines are small, lightweight charts that fit into individual cells. They allow you to see trends, variations, and highlights in data at a glance. Unlike traditional charts, sparklines are tied to the data in their corresponding rows or columns.

Types of Sparklines:

- Line Sparklines: Display trends over time.
- Column Sparklines: Highlight variations in values.
- Win/Loss Sparklines: Show positive and negative trends.

2.   USE CASES OF SPARKLINES

Sales Performance: track monthly sales trends for each product in a compact view.

Stock Prices: visualize daily or weekly fluctuations in stock prices.

Employee Attendance: highlight patterns of absences or irregular attendance across weeks.

Budget Analysis: compare spending trends across categories or months.

3.   CREATING SPARKLINES

1.   **Select the Data**:
   - » Highlight the data range you want to visualize (e.g., B2:E2).

2.   **Insert Sparklines**:
   - » Go to the **Insert** tab.
   - » In the **Sparklines** group, choose the type of sparkline: **Line**, **Column**, or **Win/Loss**.

3.   **Choose Location**:
   - » In the **Create Sparklines** dialog box, specify the cell where the sparkline will appear (e.g., F2).

4.   **Customize the Sparkline**:
   - » Select the cell containing the sparkline.
   - » Use the **Sparkline Tools > Design** tab to customize:
      - » **Style**: Change the color or design.
      - » **Markers**: Highlight specific points (e.g., high and low values).
      - » **Axis**: Adjust the vertical axis to normalize comparisons across rows.

4.   PRACTICAL EXAMPLES

Line Sparklines for Sales Trends:
   - » Data: Monthly sales figures for multiple products.
   - » Sparkline: Visualize trends in sales performance over months.

Column Sparklines for Performance Metrics:
   - » Data: Quarterly productivity scores.
   - » Sparkline: Use columns to emphasize differences in performance.

Win/Loss Sparklines for Binary Outcomes:
   - » Data: Game results (Win = 1, Loss = -1).

> » Sparkline: Represent wins as upward markers and losses as downward markers.

5. CUSTOMIZING SPARKLINES

Add Markers: highlight important points like the highest and lowest values. Go to **Sparkline Tools > Design > Show > High Point/Low Point**.

Adjust Sparkline Color: select the sparkline cell, then go to **Sparkline Tools > Design > Sparkline Color**.

Group Sparklines: group similar sparklines to apply changes uniformly. Use **Sparkline Tools > Group**.

Clear Sparklines: to remove sparklines, go to **Sparkline Tools > Clear**.

6. EXAMPLE: USING SPARKLINES TO TRACK MONTHLY SALES TRENDS

Dataset:

	A	B	C	D	E	F
1	Product	Jan	Feb	Mar	Apr	Trend
2	Product A	50	60	55	70	
3	Product B	40	45	50	55	

Steps to Add Sparklines:
> » Select the range B2:E2 for Product A. Go to **Insert > Sparklines > Line**.
> » In the **Location Range**, enter F2 and click **OK**.
> » Repeat for Product B with B3:E3 and location F3.

Result:

	A	B	C	D	E	F
1	Product	Jan	Feb	Mar	Apr	Trend
2	Product A	50	60	55	70	⟋
3	Product B	40	45	50	55	⟋

Customizations:
> » Highlight **High Points** and **Low Points** using markers.
> » Apply a contrasting sparkline color for each row.

Formatted result:

The sparklines in column F provide a clear visual of monthly sales trends, showing steady growth for Product B and a spike in sales for Product A in April.

	A	B	C	D	E	F
1	Product	Jan	Feb	Mar	Apr	Trend
2	Product A	50	60	55	70	⟋
3	Product B	40	45	50	55	⟋

IV.   INSERTING IMAGES AND SHAPES IN YOUR WORKSHEETS

Inserting images and shapes in Excel enhances the visual appeal and functionality of your worksheets. These elements can help explain data better, create interactive dashboards, and improve overall presentation.

1.   BENEFITS OF USING IMAGES AND SHAPES IN EXCEL

Visual Explanation: Use images to clarify data points or concepts.

Highlight Important Areas: Shapes like arrows and callouts can direct attention to critical parts of the worksheet.

Interactive Dashboards: Combine shapes with hyperlinks to create navigation buttons.

Branding: Insert company logos to maintain a consistent brand identity in reports.

2.   HOW TO INSERT IMAGES

Excel supports the insertion of images from various sources, including your computer and online.
Steps to Insert an Image:

1.   **Insert from File**:
   » Go to **Insert > Pictures > Place in Cell/ Place over Cells > This Device**.
   » Browse to select the image and click **Insert**.

2.   **Insert from Online**:
   » Go to **Insert > Pictures > Place in Cell/ Place over Cells > Online Pictures**.
   » Search for the desired image and insert it into the worksheet.

3.   **Resize and Position**:
   » Drag the image corners to resize while maintaining aspect ratio.
   » Click and drag the image to position it within the worksheet.

3.   HOW TO INSERT SHAPES

Shapes are versatile tools for annotating, highlighting, or enhancing worksheet design.

i.   Types of Shapes:

- **Arrows**: Indicate trends or point to key data.
- **Rectangles and Circles**: Highlight data sections.
- **Callouts**: Add notes or explanations.
- **Lines**: Separate sections or guide the viewer.

ii. Steps to Insert Shapes:

1. Go to the Insert Tab:

» Click **Insert > Shapes** and select the desired shape.

2. Draw the Shape:

» Click and drag on the worksheet to draw the shape.

3. Format the Shape:

» Use the **Shape Format** tab to:

- » Change the fill color and outline.
- » Apply effects like shadows or 3D formatting.
- » Add text inside the shape.

V. ADVANCED VISUALIZATION TOOLS: COMBO CHARTS AND DATA BARS

Advanced visualization tools like combo charts and data bars enable you to represent complex datasets effectively. They are ideal for showing relationships between multiple variables or visualizing data directly within cells.

1. COMBO CHARTS

Combo charts combine two or more chart types (e.g., bar and line charts) in a single visualization, making it easier to analyze datasets with varying types of data.

Use Cases of Combo Charts:

- **Sales and Profit Analysis**: Display total sales as bars and profit margins as a line.
- **Website Analytics**: Show page views as columns and bounce rate as a line.
- **Weather Trends**: Combine temperature data as columns and rainfall as a line.

Example:

Steps to Create a Combo Chart:

1. Select the Data:

» Highlight the dataset, including headers (e.g. A1:C5).

	A	B	C
1	Month	Sales ($)	Profit Margin
2	January	5,000	20%
3	February	7,000	25%
4	March	6,000	18%
5	April	8,000	30%

2. Insert a Combo Chart:

» Go to **Insert > Charts > Insert Combo Chart**.

» Select **Create Custom Combo Chart**.

3. Configure Chart Types:

» Assign "Sales" to a clustered column chart.

» Assign "Profit Margin" to a line chart.

» Check **Secondary Axis** for the line chart.

4. Customize the Chart:

» Add a title (e.g., "Sales and Profit Trends").

» Format the secondary axis to display percentages.

» Adjust colors to differentiate the bars and line.

Result:

Sales and Profit Trends

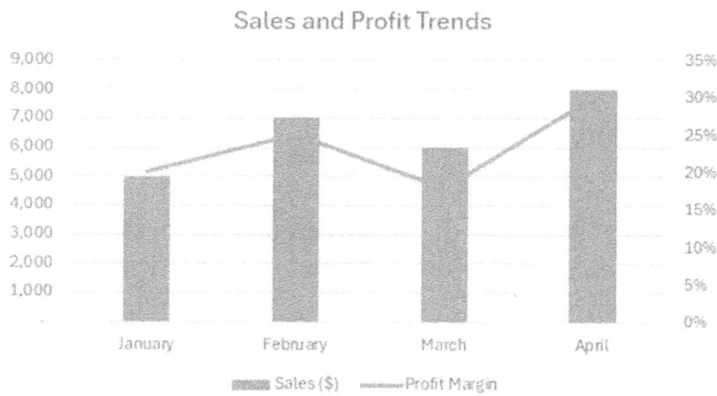

Sales ($)   Profit Margin

Tips for Combo Charts:

- Use a secondary axis for clarity when combining metrics with different scales.
- Limit to two or three data series to avoid clutter.

2. DATA BARS

Data bars are a form of conditional formatting that visually represent values directly within cells. They provide an intuitive way to compare data without creating separate charts.

Use Cases of Data Bars:

- **Sales Targets**: Highlight performance levels across regions.
- **Project Progress**: Display completion percentages for tasks.
- **Inventory Levels**: Visualize stock quantities.

Example:

Steps to Add Data Bars:

1. **Select the Data**: Highlight the range with numeric data.

	A	B
1	Region	Sales ($)
2	North	5,000
3	South	7,000
4	East	6,000
5	West	4,000

2. **Apply Conditional Formatting**:
   » Go to **Home > Conditional Formatting > Data Bars**.
   » Choose a gradient or solid fill style.

3. **Customize Data Bars**:
   » Open the **Manage Rules** dialog box under **Conditional Formatting**.
   » Adjust the minimum and maximum values if needed (e.g., set specific thresholds).

Result:

	A	B
1	Region	Sales ($)
2	North	5,000
3	South	7,000
4	East	6,000
5	West	4,000

Tips for Data Bars:

- Use solid fills for better visibility in dense datasets.
- Combine data bars with numerical values in adjacent columns for added context.

VI. USING EXCEL WITH POWER BI AND DASHBOARDS

Excel is often the starting point for deeper reporting and dashboard work. Many organizations use Excel for data preparation and analysis, then move the finished tables or models into Power BI to create interactive dashboards. This section gives you a simple overview—no advanced Power BI knowledge required.

1. HOW EXCEL AND POWER BI WORK TOGETHER

Excel connects naturally with Power BI. A few common workflows include:

- Importing Excel tables into Power BI
  » Any formatted Excel table can be brought directly into Power BI Desktop for further modeling and visualization.

- Using Power Pivot and the Data Model
  » If your workbook uses relationships, measures, or the Data Model, Power BI will read these structures and carry them forward.

- Summarizing data using PivotTables before export
  » PivotTables can prepare clean summary tables that become the starting point for dashboard visuals in Power BI.

These connections make Excel a strong "data shaping" tool before your report moves into Power BI.

2. WHEN TO USE POWER BI INSTEAD OF EXCEL

Excel remains the best tool for ad-hoc analysis, grid-based calculation, and individual reporting. Power BI becomes more useful when your needs grow, such as:

- You want interactive visuals (slicers, drill-downs, hover effects)
- You're combining multiple data sources (databases, CSVs, cloud services)
- Your audience needs a dashboard view, not a worksheet
- You need reports that update automatically from live data
- Your charts will be shared with teams rather than individuals

Think of Excel as the analysis tool, and Power BI as the presentation layer for ongoing reporting.

3. EXPORT OR PUBLISH OPTIONS

There are several ways to move your Excel work into Power BI:

- Export tables as CSV
  - » Good for small datasets and simple workflows.
- Use OneDrive or SharePoint connections
  - » Power BI can connect directly to files stored in the cloud and refresh them automatically.
- Import Excel workbooks into Power BI Desktop
  - » Ideal when your workbook already contains tables, relationships, or a Data Model.
- Pin Excel charts to Power BI dashboards
  - » Charts created in Excel can be published to Power BI and displayed as tiles inside a dashboard.

These options give you flexibility, depending on how advanced your report needs to be.

You may not need Power BI today, but knowing how Excel fits into a modern reporting workflow helps you plan ahead. Whether you stay inside Excel or move into Power BI later, the same clean data practices—tables, named ranges, relationships, and Power Query—apply in both tools.

VII. USING COPILOT TO SUPPORT VISUALIZATIONS

Copilot can assist you while creating charts and visuals, even if you only have the built-in Copilot Chat version. Copilot Chat appears in a panel on the right side of Excel and helps you understand chart types, choose the right visual, and walk through steps when you're unsure where to click.

If you have the full Microsoft 365 Copilot subscription (paid add-on), Copilot can also apply formatting, suggest visual layouts, and make changes directly to your workbook.

i. How Copilot Chat Can Help With Visualizations

Copilot Chat is especially helpful when you're deciding which chart to create or when you need instructions. You can ask it questions at any time, and it will guide you using your current data.

Example prompts:

- "What is the best chart type to compare monthly sales?"
- "Explain the difference between a bar chart and a column chart."
- "Which chart should I use to show a trend over time?"
- "How do I add data labels to this chart?"
- "How do I format only the highest values in this series?"

Copilot Chat can't click the buttons for you, but it will tell you exactly how to perform the steps.

ii. What the Full Microsoft 365 Copilot Can Do

If you have the full Copilot license, you can also ask Copilot to:

- Suggest the most appropriate chart for a selected range.
- Apply chart formatting automatically.
- Create summaries or insights from the visual.
- Highlight key points or trends.
- Build a chart based on what you describe ("Create a column chart showing total sales by region").

These features streamline your workflow and help you produce clearer visuals more quickly.

iii. When Copilot Is Most Useful

Copilot is most helpful when:

- You're unsure which chart type fits your data
- You want to adjust chart formatting but don't know where to find the settings
- Your data needs a summary before charting
- You want an explanation of why a trend or outlier appears
- You need quick guidance without leaving your worksheet

Even with Copilot Chat alone, having an AI assistant inside Excel makes visualization tasks easier to learn and understand.

CHAPTER 6:
INTERMEDIATE EXCEL SKILLS

I. WORKING WITH NAMED RANGES

Named ranges in Excel simplify formulas, enhance readability, and make managing large datasets more efficient. A named range is a custom label assigned to a cell or group of cells, allowing you to reference it easily in formulas or other operations.

1. BENEFITS OF USING NAMED RANGES

Improved Formula Clarity:
Instead of referencing cells like A1:A10, you can use a descriptive name like SalesData.

Easier Data Management:
Named ranges simplify navigating and maintaining large datasets.

Dynamic Updates:
Named ranges can adapt dynamically to changes in data when defined as dynamic ranges.

2. HOW TO CREATE NAMED RANGES

1. **Select the Cells**:
    » Highlight the cells you want to name (e.g., A1:A10).

2. **Name the Range**:
    » Go to the **Formulas** tab and click **Define Name** in the **Defined Names** group.
    » Enter a descriptive name (e.g., SalesData) in the **New Name** dialog box and click **OK**.

3. **Verify the Range**:
    » Use the **Name Manager** under the **Formulas** tab to view, edit, or delete named ranges.

3. USING NAMED RANGES IN FORMULAS

Named ranges can replace cell references in formulas, making them easier to understand.

Example: We have the dataset as below:

Create a Named Range:

	A	B
1	Month	Sales ($)
2	January	5,000
3	February	7,000
4	March	6,000

» Select the range B2:B4 and name it MonthlySales.

1. **Use the Named Range in a Formula**:

» Calculate the total sales:
=SUM(MonthlySales)

» Returns: 18,000

2. **Dynamic Named Range**:

» Use formulas to define a range that expands automatically as data is added.

» Example:
Go to **Formulas > Define Name**, and for the range, enter:
=OFFSET(Sheet1!$B$2, 0, 0, COUNTA(Sheet1!$B$2:$B$100), 1)

» This dynamic range adjusts as new data is entered in column B.

4. MANAGING NAMED RANGES

View or Edit Named Ranges:

» Go to **Formulas > Name Manager** to see all named ranges.

» Select a name and click **Edit** to modify it or **Delete** to remove it.

Use Named Ranges Across Sheets:

» Named ranges are workbook-wide, meaning they can be used in formulas across different sheets.

Apply Scope to Named Ranges:

» When creating a named range, set the scope to a specific sheet or the entire workbook.

5. PRACTICAL APPLICATIONS OF NAMED RANGES

Sales Reporting:

» Use named ranges like ProductSales to simplify aggregation formulas.

» Example: =AVERAGE(ProductSales) calculates the average sales.

Financial Modeling:

» Replace hard-coded cell references with meaningful names like InterestRate or LoanAmount.

» Example: =LoanAmount*InterestRate makes formulas intuitive.

Dynamic Dashboards:

» Use named ranges with charts to automatically update visualizations when data changes.

Conditional Formatting:

> » Apply named ranges to create dynamic rules for formatting datasets.

II. CREATING AND MANAGING PIVOT TABLES

Pivot tables are one of Excel's most powerful features, enabling you to summarize, analyze, and extract insights from large datasets efficiently. They allow you to rearrange, group, and filter data dynamically without altering the original dataset.

1. WHAT ARE PIVOT TABLES?

A pivot table is an interactive table that summarizes data by aggregating values (e.g., sum, average, count) and grouping them into categories. It helps users analyze trends, patterns, and relationships within the data.

Use Cases:

- **Sales Analysis**: Summarize revenue by product, region, or salesperson.
- **Inventory Management**: Track stock levels by category and supplier.
- **Survey Analysis**: Count responses for different questions by demographic.

2. STEPS TO CREATE A PIVOT TABLE (WITH EXAMPLE)

Example Dataset

	A	B	C	D	E
1	Region	Product	Salesperson	Sales ($)	Date
2	North	Widget A	Alice	500	01-Jan-24
3	South	Widget B	Bob	700	02-Jan-24
4	East	Widget A	Alice	600	03-Jan-24
5	West	Widget C	Charlie	400	04-Jan-24
6	North	Widget B	Alice	800	05-Jan-24

1. **Select the Data**
   > » Highlight the dataset (A1:E6), including headers.
   > » Go to **Insert > PivotTable**.

2. **Configure the Pivot Table**
   > » In the **Create PivotTable** dialog box:
   >> » Select **New Worksheet** or **Existing Worksheet** for the table location. Click **OK**.
   > » In the **PivotTable Field List** pane: drag fields to different areas:
   >> » **Rows**: Region

> » **Columns**: Product
> » **Values**: Sales ($) (set to Sum by default)
> » **Filters**: Salesperson

3. Analyze the Results

	A	B	C	D	E	F	G	H	I	J	K
1	Region	Product	Salesperson	Sales ($)	Date		Salesperson	(All)			
2	North	Widget A	Alice	500	01-Jan-24						
3	South	Widget B	Bob	700	02-Jan-24		Sum of Sales ($)	Column Labels			
4	East	Widget A	Alice	600	03-Jan-24		Row Labels	Widget A	Widget B	Widget C	Grand Total
5	West	Widget C	Charlie	400	04-Jan-24		East	600			600
6	North	Widget B	Alice	800	05-Jan-24		North	500	800		1,300
7							South		700		700
8							West			400	400
9			Filter to view				**Grand Total**	1,100	1,500	400	3,000
10			each salesperson								

The pivot table summarizes sales by region and product. Use the filter dropdown to view data for specific salespeople.

3. MANAGING PIVOT TABLES

Updating the Data:
> » If the source data changes, click the pivot table.
> » Go to **PivotTable Analyze > Refresh** to update.

Grouping Data:
> » Right-click on a field (e.g., Date) and select **Group**.
> » Choose how to group (e.g., by months, quarters, or years).

Adding Calculated Fields:
> » Go to **PivotTable Analyze > Fields, Items & Sets > Calculated Field**.
> » Define a formula using existing fields. Example: Add a "Profit" field with the formula =Sales * 0.2.

Sorting and Filtering:
> » Use the dropdown arrows in the row or column headers to sort or filter data.
> » Apply filters in the **Filters** area to analyze subsets of data.

4. TIPS FOR USING PIVOT TABLES

Use Slicers for Dynamic Filtering:
> » Add slicers to filter data visually.

» Go to **PivotTable Analyze > Insert Slicer**.

Apply Conditional Formatting:
 » Highlight key values in the pivot table for better visualization.
 » Select data, then go to **Home > Conditional Formatting**.

Summarize with Different Functions:
 » Change the aggregation type (e.g., Average, Max, Count).
 » Right-click a value field, select **Summarize Values By**, and choose the function.

Use Multiple Tables:
 » Combine data from multiple sheets using Power Pivot for advanced analysis.

III. USING SLICERS FOR DYNAMIC DATA ANALYSIS

Slicers are an advanced filtering tool in Excel that provide a user-friendly way to dynamically analyze data in pivot tables and tables. They allow you to filter datasets visually by clicking buttons, making them ideal for creating interactive dashboards and reports.

1. WHAT ARE SLICERS?

Slicers are graphical filters that display clickable buttons to filter data dynamically. Unlike traditional dropdown filters, slicers are more intuitive and visually appealing, especially when analyzing large datasets or sharing reports with others.

Benefits of Using Slicers

- **Interactive Filtering**: Quickly filter pivot tables and tables by clicking buttons.
- **Ease of Use**: No need to open dropdown menus; filters are applied instantly.
- **Multiple Filters**: Apply filters to multiple pivot tables or tables simultaneously.
- **Professional Dashboards**: Enhance the interactivity and visual appeal of dashboards.

2. STEPS TO CREATE AND USE SLICERS (WITH EXAMPLE)

Example Dataset

1. **Create a Pivot Table**
 » Highlight the dataset and go to **Insert > PivotTable**.
 » Configure the pivot table:
   » **Rows**: Add Region.

	A	B	C	D	E
1	Region	Product	Salesperson	Sales ($)	Date
2	North	Widget A	Alice	500	01-Jan-24
3	South	Widget B	Bob	700	02-Jan-24
4	East	Widget A	Alice	600	03-Jan-24
5	West	Widget C	Charlie	400	04-Jan-24
6	North	Widget B	Alice	800	05-Jan-24

» **Columns**: Add Product.

» **Values**: Add Sales ($).

2. **Insert a Slicer**

» Select the pivot table.

» Go to **PivotTable Analyze > Insert Slicer**.

» Choose fields to filter by (e.g., Region, Product, or Salesperson).

» Click **OK** to insert the slicer.

3. **Use the Slicer**

» Click buttons on the slicer to filter data dynamically.

» To select multiple items, hold Ctrl while clicking the buttons.

» Use the clear filter icon in the slicer to remove all filters.

Sum of Sales ($)	Column Labels ▾				Region
Row Labels ▾	Widget A	Widget B	Widget C	Grand Total	
East	600			600	East
North	500	800		1,300	North
South		700		700	
West			400	400	South
Grand Total	1,100	1,500	400	3,000	West

3. CUSTOMIZING SLICERS

Resize and Move Slicers:

» Drag the slicer to reposition it on the worksheet. Resize it by dragging the edges.

Change Slicer Style:

» Go to **Slicer Tools > Options > Slicer Styles** and choose a preformatted style.

Adjust Button Layout:

» Under **Slicer Tools > Options > Buttons**, adjust the number of columns and button size.

Connect to Multiple Pivot Tables:

» Select the slicer, go to **Slicer Tools > Options > Report Connections**, and link it to multiple pivot tables.

4. TIPS FOR USING SLICERS

Group Related Filters: Place slicers close to related pivot tables for easy access.

Use Descriptive Titles: Rename slicers to clarify their purpose (e.g., "Filter by Region").

Combine with Conditional Formatting: Highlight filtered data in pivot tables for better visualization.

Limit Overlapping Filters: Avoid applying too many slicers that could conflict or confuse users.

IV.   INTRODUCTION TO POWER QUERY

Power Query is a data transformation and automation tool built into Excel. It allows you to connect, clean, and transform data from various sources without manual intervention. By mastering Power Query, you can streamline data preparation and improve efficiency in your workflows.

1.   WHAT IS POWER QUERY?

Power Query simplifies importing and transforming data. It works through an intuitive interface where you can clean, reshape, and combine data from various sources like text files, databases, or web pages, all without needing advanced coding skills.

Key Features:

- Connects to multiple data sources (Excel files, databases, web, APIs).
- Automates repetitive data-cleaning tasks.
- Supports advanced transformations like merging, unpivoting, and splitting columns.

Benefits of Using Power Query

- **Automation**: save time by automating repetitive data-cleaning steps.
- **Integration**: combine data from multiple sources into a unified format.
- **Consistency**: apply the same transformation logic to ensure data accuracy.
- **Ease of Use**: no coding required; use an intuitive point-and-click interface.

2.   EXAMPLE CLEANING AND COMBINING DATA WITH POWER QUERY

Scenario: You have monthly sales data stored in separate files, and you want to combine them into a single table while removing duplicates and formatting columns.

Files: 2 files named January Sales and February Sales with data as below:

	A	B	C
1	Month	Region	Sales ($)
2	January	North	500
3	January	South	700

	A	B	C
1	Month	Region	Sales ($)
2	January	North	500
3	January	South	700
4	February	North	600
5	February	South	800

Steps to Combine Data:

1. **Connect to Data Sources**:

   » Go to **Data > Get Data > From Folder**.

   » Select the folder where you store January and February sales files.

2. **Combine Data:**

   » Select Combine & Load

   » In the Combine Files dialog box, select Sheet1. Click OK.

Result:

	A	B	C	D
1	Source.Name	Month	Region	Sales ($)
2	February Sales.xlsx	January	North	500
3	February Sales.xlsx	January	South	700
4	February Sales.xlsx	February	North	600
5	February Sales.xlsx	February	South	800
6	January Sales.xlsx	January	North	500
7	January Sales.xlsx	January	South	700

Steps to Clean Data:

   » Select a cell in the combined data, then go to **Query > Edit** to open Power Query Editor.

   » Remove duplicate rows: select the column you want to remove duplicates from, then go to **Home > Remove Duplicates**.

   » Group By: for more complicated data, Group By function works better to remove duplicates.

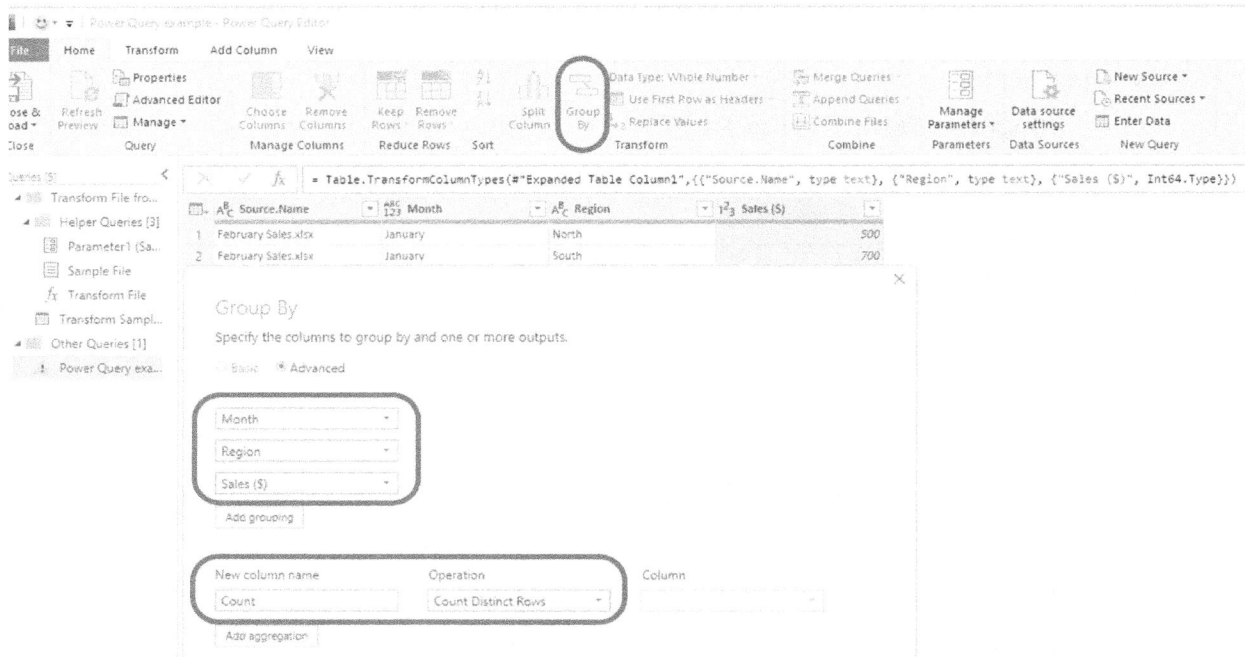

» Remove unnecessary columns: select the column, then go to **Home > Remove Columns.**

» Rename columns: Double-click column headers to rename them for clarity.

» Result:

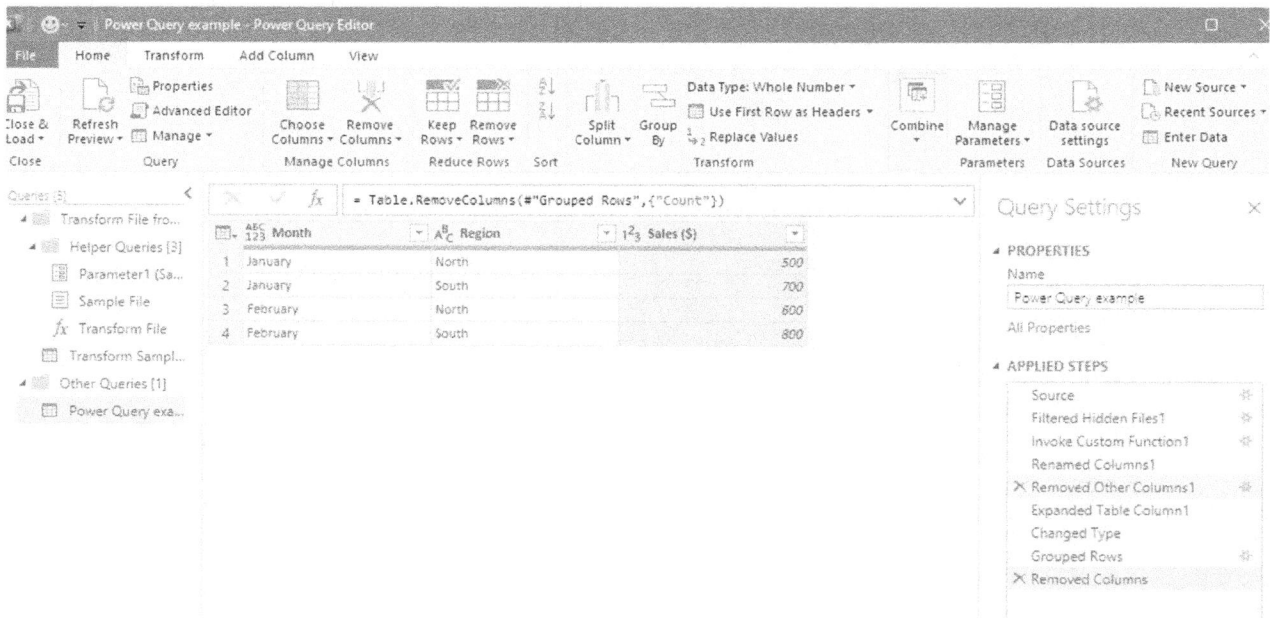

3. **Load Data into Excel**:

» Once cleaned, click **Close & Load**. The previous table will be updated with duplicates removed.

Result:

	A	B	C
1	Month	Region	Sales ($)
2	January	North	500
3	January	South	700
4	February	North	600
5	February	South	800

3. COMMON TRANSFORMATIONS IN POWER QUERY

Filtering Rows: remove unnecessary rows by applying filters, such as excluding blanks or values outside a range.

Splitting Columns: divide data in one column into multiple columns based on delimiters (e.g., commas or spaces).

Merging Queries: combine data from two tables using a common key (e.g., Region or Product ID).

Unpivoting Columns: transform wide datasets into long-format tables for easier analysis.

Grouping Data: aggregate data by categories, such as summing sales by region.

4. PRACTICAL APPLICATIONS

Sales Reporting: import monthly sales data from multiple CSV files and clean it for analysis.

Inventory Management: merge inventory lists from suppliers into a single table and filter out discontinued items.

Survey Analysis: combine survey responses from various sources and pivot data for analysis.

Data Preparation for Dashboards: create a clean and dynamic dataset that automatically updates when source files change.

5. TIPS FOR USING POWER QUERY

Save Queries: save your queries for reuse, especially when working with frequently updated data.

Use Parameters: create parameters for dynamic filtering or paths, like selecting a specific year or file location.

Preview Changes: use the preview pane in Power Query Editor to verify transformations before loading data.

Document Steps: Power Query keeps a step-by-step log of all transformations, ensuring transparency and repeatability.

V. BASIC MACROS: AUTOMATING REPETITIVE TASKS

Macros in Excel allow you to automate repetitive tasks by recording a sequence of actions and replaying them with a single click or shortcut. Learning to use macros is a significant step toward improving productivity and mastering Excel's advanced capabilities.

1. WHAT ARE MACROS?

A macro is a set of recorded instructions that automates routine tasks in Excel. Macros are written in VBA (Visual Basic for Applications), but Excel provides a user-friendly recorder for those unfamiliar with coding.

Common Use Cases:

- Automating formatting across multiple sheets.
- Performing repetitive calculations or updates.
- Generating reports with standardized layouts.
- Consolidating data from multiple files.

2. ENABLING MACROS IN EXCEL

By default, Excel disables macros for security reasons. To use them:

1. Go to **File > Options > Trust Center > Trust Center Settings**.
2. Select **Macro Settings** and enable **Enable all macros** or **Disable all macros with notification**.
3. Click **OK** to save changes.

3. RECORDING A MACRO

Excel's Macro Recorder simplifies automation by recording actions without requiring you to write code.

Steps to Record a Macro:

1. **Start Recording**:
   » Go to **View > Macros > Record Macro**.
   » Name the macro (e.g., FormatReport) and assign a shortcut key (optional).
   » Choose where to store the macro:
       » **This Workbook**: Macro is saved only in the current workbook.
       » **Personal Macro Workbook**: Macro is available in all workbooks.
2. **Perform the Actions**: carry out the tasks you want to automate (e.g., formatting a table, applying formulas).
3. **Stop Recording**: go to **View > Macros > Stop Recording**.

4. RUNNING A MACRO

To run a recorded macro:

1. Go to **View > Macros > View Macros**.
2. Select the macro from the list and click **Run**.

Alternatively, use the assigned shortcut key to execute the macro instantly.

5. EDITING AND MANAGING MACROS

Viewing Macro Code:
- » Go to **View > Macros > View Macros**.
- » Select a macro and click **Edit** to view the VBA code in the editor.

Deleting a Macro:
- » Open **View > Macros > View Macros**.
- » Select the macro and click **Delete**.

Saving a Workbook with Macros:
- » Save the workbook as a **Macro-Enabled Workbook** (.xlsm) to retain macros.
- » Go to **File > Save As** and choose **Excel Macro-Enabled Workbook** from the file type dropdown.

6. EXAMPLE: FORMATTING A SALES REPORT

We will use dataset below for our example (Table 1):

	A	B
1	**Region**	**Sales ($)**
2	North	5,000
3	South	7,000
4	East	6,000
5	West	4,000

Formatting tasks:
- » Bold the headers.
- » Apply currency formatting to the Sales column.
- » Add a total row using =SUM(B2:B5).

Steps to format:
- » Go to **View > Macros > Record Macro**.
- » Name the macro as FormatReport and store the macro in current workbook.
- » Select A1: B1 and bold it. Use arrow down key to select B2: B5 and press Ctrl+1 to format currency.
- » Use arrow keys to go to cell A5, click on **Macros > Use Relative References** to go to cell A6, type in Total.
- » Use arrow right key to go to cell B6, type in =SUM($B$2:B5)
- » To stop recording, go to **Macros > Stop Recording**.

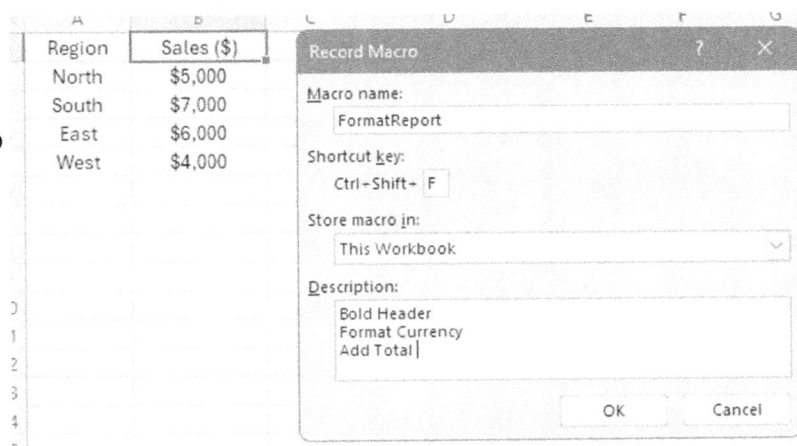

To repeat the same steps for other sales reports (Table 2), we can now run our Recorded Macros.

Run the macros::

» Go to **View > Macros > View Macros**.

» Select FormatReport and click Run.

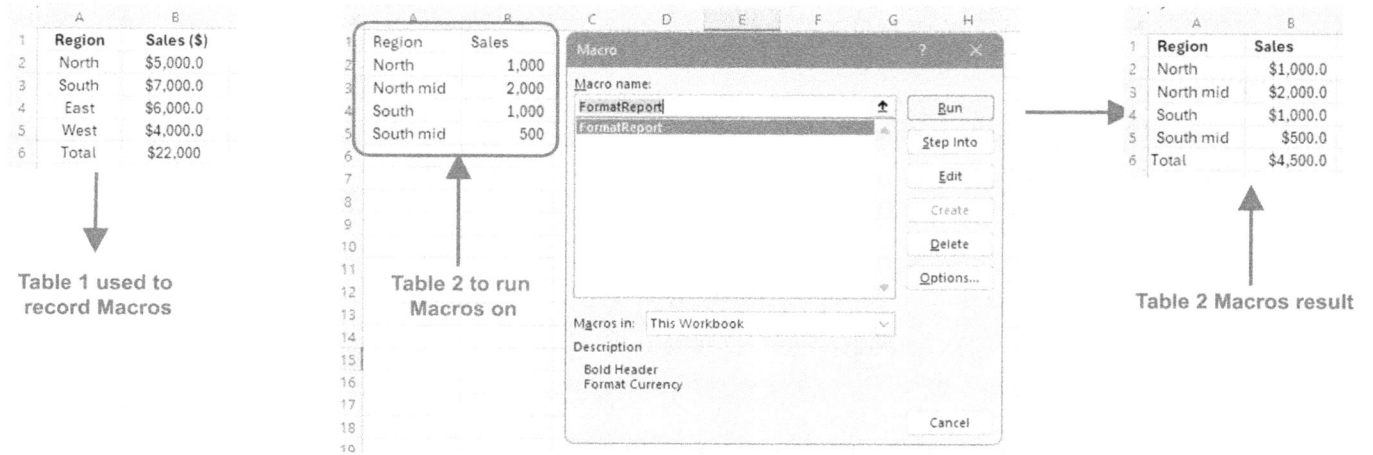

	A	B
1	**Region**	**Sales ($)**
2	North	$5,000.0
3	South	$7,000.0
4	East	$6,000.0
5	West	$4,000.0
6	Total	$22,000

Table 1 used to record Macros

	A	B
1	Region	Sales
2	North	1,000
3	North mid	2,000
4	South	1,000
5	South mid	500

Table 2 to run Macros on

Macro

Macro name:
FormatReport
FormatReport

Macros in: This Workbook
Description
Bold Header
Format Currency

Run
Step Into
Edit
Create
Delete
Options...
Cancel

	A	B
1	Region	Sales
2	North	$1,000.0
3	North mid	$2,000.0
4	South	$1,000.0
5	South mid	$500.0
6	Total	$4,500.0

Table 2 Macros result

CHAPTER 7:
ADVANCED EXCEL TECHNIQUES

I. ADVANCED FORMULAS: INDEX, MATCH, INDIRECT AND NESTED FUNCTIONS

Advanced Excel formulas like **INDEX**, **MATCH**, and **INDIRECT**, when combined with nested functions, allow you to perform powerful, efficient, and dynamic calculations. These formulas excel in scenarios requiring flexibility, dynamic range references, and advanced lookups, providing solutions that surpass basic functions like **VLOOKUP** or **SUMIFS**.

1. INDEX FUNCTION

The **INDEX** function retrieves the value of a cell within a specified range based on its row and column position. It is highly versatile and can handle both two-dimensional arrays (tables) and one-dimensional arrays (rows or columns). The function supports two syntaxes: array form and reference form.

i. Array form

Syntax:
=INDEX(array, row_num, [column_num])

Understanding the Arguments

- **array**: the range of cells or array from which to retrieve data.
- **row_num**: the row number in the array to retrieve data from.
- **column_num**: (Optional) the column number in the array to retrieve data from.

ii. Reference form

Syntax:
=INDEX(reference, row_num, [column_num], [area_num])

Understanding the Arguments

- **reference**: Multiple ranges or areas separated by commas. Example: (A1:A3, B1:B3).
- **row_num**: The row number in the selected range.
- **[column_num]** (optional): The column number in the selected range. Defaults to the first column if omitted.

- **[area_num]** (optional): Specifies which range (or area) to use when multiple areas are provided. Defaults to the first range if omitted.

iii. Differences between Array form and Reference form

Feature	Array Form	Reference Form
Range	Single range or array	Multiple ranges (non-contiguous areas)
Flexibility	Simplified lookup	Supports dynamic selection of ranges
Complexity	Less complex, easier to use	Slightly more advanced, requires area_num
Primary Use Case	Row and column lookups within a table	Dynamic range selection for larger datasets

When to Use Each Syntax

- Array Form: When working with a single, contiguous dataset. Ideal for straightforward lookups and simple formulas.
- Reference Form: When dealing with multiple datasets or ranges, or when you need dynamic flexibility in selecting a range.

iv. Examples

We will use below dataset for our examples.

Task: Find the price of the second product.

> Formula: =INDEX(A2:D5, 2, 4)
> The formula asks Excel to find the value in range A2:D5, second row and fourth column.
> Result: 75

Task: Find the store manager of the second store.

> Formula: =INDEX((A2:D5, A8:C11), 2, 3, 2)
> The formula asks Excel to find value in 2 ranges A2:D5 (range 1) and A8:C11 (range 2), second row and third column of range 2.
> Result: Bob

	A	B	C	D
1	Product ID	Product Name	Category	Price ($)
2	101	Widget A	Electronics	50
3	102	Widget B	Electronics	75
4	103	Widget C	Home Appliances	100
5	104	Widget D	Home Appliances	125
6				
7	Store	Region	Manager	
8	Downtown	North	Alice	
9	Uptown	South	Bob	
10	Suburb	East	Carol	
11	City Center	West	David	

Use Cases:

- **Basic Lookup**: Retrieve specific data from a range.
- **Dynamic Row Selection**: Select rows dynamically based on criteria.
- **Error-Free Lookup**: Avoid errors caused by column order changes in **VLOOKUP**.
- **Dynamic Data Retrieval**: Pull specific data from tables or arrays.
- **Combining with MATCH**: Use INDEX with MATCH for powerful lookups.
- **Handling Multiple Ranges**: Reference different areas dynamically with area_num.

2. MATCH FUNCTION

The **MATCH** function finds the relative position of a value within a range. It is often used in combination with **INDEX** for flexible and dynamic lookups.

Syntax:
=MATCH(lookup_value, lookup_array, [match_type])

Understanding the Arguments

- **lookup_value**: The value to search for.
- **lookup_array**: The range to search in.
- **match_type**: 0 for an exact match, 1 for the largest value less than or equal to the lookup value, -1 for the smallest value greater than or equal to the lookup value.

Use Cases:

- **Find Position in a List**: Identify the position of a specific product or value.
- **Dynamic Row or Column Reference**: Use the result of **MATCH** to dynamically locate rows or columns in other formulas.

Example:

Task: Find the position of Widget C in column B.

> » Formula: =MATCH("Widget C",B1:B5,0). Result: 4.

	A	B	C	D
1	Product ID	Product Name	Category	Price ($)
2	101	Widget A	Electronics	50
3	102	Widget B	Electronics	75
4	103	Widget C	Home Appliances	100
5	104	Widget D	Home Appliances	125
6				

Task: Find the position of Widget C in row 4.

> » Formula: =MATCH("Widget C", A4:D4,0). Result: 2.

3. COMBINING INDEX AND MATCH

The combination of **INDEX** and **MATCH** provides a more robust solution than **VLOOKUP**, allowing for dynamic lookups in both rows and columns.

Advantages Over VLOOKUP:

- **Flexible Column Selection**: Unlike **VLOOKUP**, which requires the lookup column to be the first column, **INDEX** and **MATCH** can work with data in any order.
- **Error Resilience**: They are not affected by column insertions or deletions.
- **Performance**: Faster in large datasets.

Use Cases:

- **Two-Dimensional Lookup**: Retrieve data based on both row and column criteria.
- **Dynamic Dashboards**: Build interactive dashboards where users can select lookup criteria.

Example:

Task: Find the price for Widget C.

	A	B	C	D
1	Product ID	Product Name	Category	Price ($)
2	101	Widget A	Electronics	50
3	102	Widget B	Electronics	75
4	103	Widget C	Home Appliances	100
5	104	Widget D	Home Appliances	125
6				

- » Formula:
  =INDEX(D1:D5,MATCH("Widget C",B1:B5,0))
- » The formula asks Excel to find the value in range D1:D5, row number is whichever position Widget C is in range B1:B5.
- » Result: 100.

4. INDIRECT FUNCTION

The **INDIRECT** function dynamically references ranges based on a text string. It is particularly useful for creating dynamic, flexible formulas.

Syntax:
=INDIRECT(ref_text, [a1])

Understanding the Arguments

- **ref_text**: A text string representing a cell or range reference.
- **a1**: (Optional) TRUE for A1-style references, FALSE for R1C1-style references.

Use Cases:

- **Dynamic Range References**: Switch ranges based on user inputs or dropdown selections.
- **Flexible Consolidation**: Combine data from multiple sheets without manually updating formulas.
- **Shortening Complex Formulas**: Simplify long **VLOOKUP** or **SUMIFS** formulas with dynamic ranges.

Examples: We will use dataset below for our examples.

	A	B	C	D	E
1	Salesperson	Region	Jan Sales ($)	Feb Sales ($)	Mar Sales ($)
2	Alice	North	500	600	550
3	Bob	South	450	700	800
4	Carol	East	700	750	720
5	David	West	600	500	650
6					
7	Region	Target ($)			
8	North	1,500			
9	South	2,000			
10	East	2,000			
11	West	1,800			

Simple Use Case: Referencing a Cell Address

Task: Retrieve the sales for Alice in January.
  - » Formula: =INDIRECT("C2")
  - » "C2" references the cell where Alice's January sales data is stored.
  - » Result: 500.

Dynamic Range Reference

Task: Retrieve total sales for Bob using a dynamically constructed range.
  - » Formula: =SUM(INDIRECT("C3:E3"))
  - » "C3:E3" dynamically constructs the range covering Bob's sales for January to March.
  - » Result: 1,950.

Combining INDIRECT with SUM and IF

Task: Compare a region's total sales to its target dynamically.
  - » Formula: =IF(SUM(INDIRECT("C"&MATCH('North",B1:B5,0)&"
    E"&MATCH("North",B1:B5,0))) >= INDIRECT("B"&MATCH("North",A8:A11,0)+7), "Met
    Target", "Below Target")
  - » MATCH("North",B1:B5,0): Finds the row number for "North" in the first table (row 2).
  - » INDIRECT("C"&MATCH("North",B1:B5,0)&":E"&MATCH("North",B1:B5,0)): Dynamically
    references the sales data range for the "North" region (C2:E2).
  - » INDIRECT("B"&MATCH("North",A8:A11,0)+7): Dynamically references the sales target
    for the "North" region from the second table.
  - » Result: Met Target.

II.   GOAL SEEK

1.   WHAT IS GOAL SEEK?

Goal Seek is part of Excel's **What-If Analysis** tools. It works by adjusting a single input value in a formula to achieve a desired output.

Use Cases:

- **Financial Modeling**: Determine the required sales to meet a profit target.
- **Loan Calculations**: Find the interest rate or term to meet a specific monthly payment.
- **Break-Even Analysis**: Calculate the required units to break even.
- **Pricing Strategy**: Identify the optimal price to hit revenue goals.

2.   HOW GOAL SEEK WORKS

Goal Seek requires three inputs:

- **Set Cell**: The cell containing the formula or value you want to achieve.
- **To Value**: The target value you want the set cell to achieve.
- **By Changing Cell**: The input cell that Excel will adjust to achieve the target.

3.   EXAMPLE

Scenario: Determine the Required Sales to Meet a Profit Target

	A	B	C	D	E	F
1	Product	Price ($)	Units Sold	Total Revenue ($)	Costs ($)	Profit ($)
2	Widget A	50	100	5,000	3,000	2,000

Goal: Adjust **Units Sold** to achieve a profit of **$3,000**.

Steps:

1. **Set Up the Formula**:
   » Calculate **Total Revenue**: =Price * Units Sold
   » Calculate **Costs**: = Unit Cost * Units Sold. From the data given, we know the Unit Cost is $30 per unit.
   » Calculate **Profit**: =Total Revenue - Costs

2. **Access Goal Seek**:
   » Go to **Data > What-If Analysis > Goal Seek**.

3. **Enter Goal Seek Parameters**:

» **Set Cell**: Select the Profit cell (F2).

» **To Value**: Enter 3000.

» **By Changing Cell**: Select the Units Sold cell (C2).

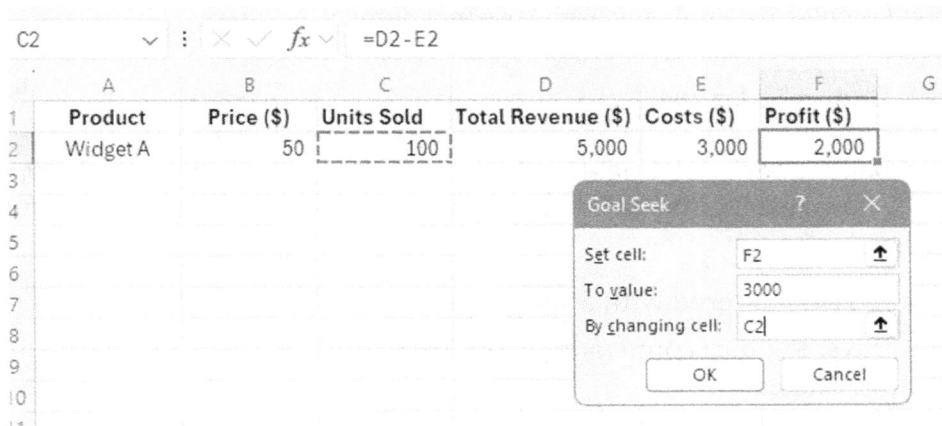

4. **Run Goal Seek**:

» Excel adjusts the **Units Sold** value to 150 to meet the profit target.

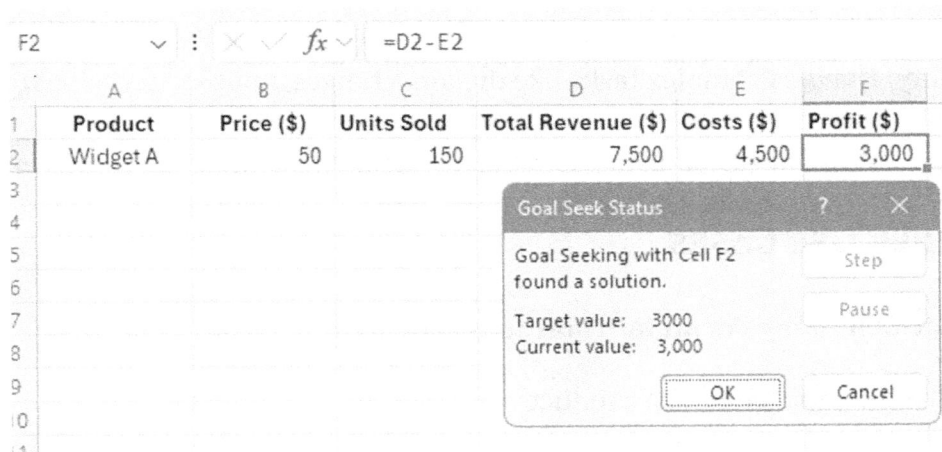

III. USING ARRAY FORMULAS

Array formulas in Excel are powerful tools that enable calculations on multiple values simultaneously. They can process data arrays (a single column, row, or a combination of both) to return either a single result or multiple results. With the introduction of dynamic arrays in Excel (Microsoft 365 and Excel 2021), array formulas have become easier to use and more versatile, offering a wide range of practical applications.

1. WHAT ARE ARRAY FORMULAS?

Array formulas operate on arrays rather than individual values. They allow you to perform multiple calculations in a single formula, simplifying complex tasks like conditional aggregations, generating dynamic ranges, or creating multi-dimensional datasets.

There are two types of array formulas:

- **Single-Cell Array Formula**: Performs calculations and returns a single result.
  Example: Summing sales based on conditions.
- **Multi-Cell Array Formula**: Performs calculations and outputs multiple results across a range of cells.
  Example: Calculating totals for each row in a dataset.

Key Changes with Dynamic Arrays

Beginning with the September 2018 update for Microsoft 365, Excel introduced dynamic arrays, which automatically spill results into adjacent cells without requiring manual input or range selection.

- **Dynamic Arrays**: Entered with a simple press of the Enter key.
- **Legacy Arrays**: Require confirming with Ctrl + Shift + Enter (CSE) and manual selection of the output range.

Advantages of Array Formulas

- Consistency: A single array formula applies the same logic across all calculations.
- Efficiency: Reduces the need for intermediate formulas, leading to smaller file sizes.
- Flexibility: Handles complex tasks like dynamic ranges, multi-criteria lookups, or condition-based calculations.
- Updates: Automatically adjusts when the source data changes (with dynamic arrays).

2.   EXAMPLE USE CASES

Scenario 1: Multi-Cell Array Formula: Total Sales per Item

Goal: Calculate the total sales for each product.
  » Formula: =B2:B4*C2:C4
  » Enter the formula and press **Ctrl + Shift + Enter** (if using traditional arrays).
  » Result: Spills the results into adjacent cells:
    » Widget A: 50.
    » Widget B: 105.
    » Widget C: 180.

	A	B	C
1	Product	Units Sold	Unit Price ($)
2	Widget A	10	5
3	Widget B	15	7
4	Widget C	20	9

D2   ✓ ⋮ × ✓ *fx* ✓   =B2:B4*C2:C4

	A	B	C	D
1	Product	Units Sold	Unit Price ($)	Total Sales ($)
2	Widget A	10	5	50
3	Widget B	15	7	105
4	Widget C	20	9	180
5				

Scenario 2: Single-Cell Array Formula: Grand Total Sales

We use the same dataset in scenario 1.

  » Formula (Dynamic Array): =SUM(B2:B4*C2:C4)
  » Result: 335.

| | | D5 | | : | × ✓ | fx ∨ | =SUM(B2:B4*C2:C4) |

	A	B	C	D
	Product	Units Sold	Unit Price ($)	Total Sales ($)
2	Widget A	10	5	50
3	Widget B	15	7	105
4	Widget C	20	9	180
5			Grand Total	335

Scenario 3: Extracting Unique Values (Dynamic Arrays)

Goal: Extract unique regions from the dataset.

  » Formula: =UNIQUE(A1:A4)
  » Result: Spills the unique values: North, South, East.

	A
1	Region
2	North
3	South
4	North
5	East

| | B2 | | : | × ✓ | fx ∨ | =UNIQUE(A2:A5) |

	A	B	C	D
1	Region	Unique		
2	North	North		
3	South	South		
4	North	East		
5	East			

Scenario 4: Dynamic Ranges with SEQUENCE

Goal: Generate a list of numbers from 1 to 10 in a single step.

  » Formula: =SEQUENCE(10)
  » Enter the formula in one cell. Excel spills numbers 1–10 into adjacent cells automatically.

3.   LIMITATIONS OF ARRAY FORMULAS

Performance: large datasets or complex formulas may slow down calculations.

Legacy Versions: older Excel versions require **Ctrl + Shift + Enter**, which can confuse users.

Complexity: array formulas can be challenging to understand and debug.

Array formulas, particularly with the advent of dynamic arrays, have transformed how Excel handles calculations. They allow for powerful, efficient, and flexible data analysis, enabling both novice and advanced users to solve complex problems with ease. While they come with a learning curve, mastering array formulas opens up a world of possibilities in Excel.

IV. ADVANCED PIVOT TABLE TECHNIQUES: GROUPING, CALCULATED FIELDS

Pivot tables are a versatile tool for summarizing and analyzing large datasets. Advanced techniques like grouping and calculated fields can enhance their power, allowing for more detailed analysis.

1. GROUPING DATA IN PIVOT TABLES

Grouping data helps you organize and analyze large datasets by clustering values into meaningful categories, such as grouping dates into months or years, or numerical data into ranges.

Use Cases:

- **Date Grouping**: Summarize sales data by specific periods.
- **Numeric Grouping**: Group income ranges into categories (e.g., $0–$10,000, $10,001–$20,000).
- **Custom Grouping**: Combine specific items into custom groups (e.g., grouping regions into larger territories).

Example Dataset:

	A	B	C
1	Date	Region	Sales ($)
2	1/1/2024	North	500
3	1/2/2024	South	700
4	2/15/2024	East	600
5	2/20/2024	West	400
6	3/10/2024	North	800

Steps for Grouping Data:

1. **Create a Pivot Table**:
   » Highlight the dataset and go to **Insert > PivotTable**.
   » Place **Sales** in Rows and **Region** in Values.

Date	Region	Sales ($)		Row Labels	Count of Region
1/1/2024	North	500		400	1
1/2/2024	South	700		500	1
2/15/2024	East	600		600	1
2/20/2024	West	400		700	1
3/10/2024	North	800		800	1
				Grand Total	5

PivotTable Fields

Choose fields to add to report:

Search

- ☐ Date
- ☑ Region
- ☑ Sales ($)

Drag fields between areas below:

▼ Filters   ⬛ Columns

☰ Rows   Σ Values
Sales ($)   Count of Region

2. **Group Numeric Data:**
   » Right-click a value and choose **Group**.
   » Enter range intervals (e.g., Start: 0, End: 1000, By: 500).

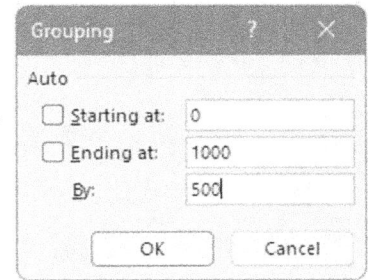

Result:
   » The data is now grouped into 2 groups.

	A	B	C	D	E	F
1	Date	Region	Sales ($)		Row Labels ▾	Count of Region
2	1/1/2024	North	500		0-499	1
3	1/2/2024	South	700		500-1000	4
4	2/15/2024	East	600		**Grand Total**	**5**
5	2/20/2024	West	400			
6	3/10/2024	North	800			

2.   USING CALCULATED FIELDS

A **calculated field** is a custom formula you define within the pivot table that is based on existing data. It allows you to add new metrics without altering the original dataset.

Use Cases:

- **Profit Calculation**: Add a calculated field for profit (e.g., Sales - Costs).
- **Profit Margin**: Calculate profit as a percentage of sales.
- **Custom Ratios**: Create metrics like sales per region or average sales per quarter.

Example Dataset:

Steps to Add a Calculated Field:

1. **Create a Pivot Table:**
   » Place Region in Rows and Sales and Costs in Values.

	A	B	C	D
1	Product	Region	Sales ($)	Costs ($)
2	Widget A	North	500	300
3	Widget B	South	700	400
4	Widget C	East	600	350

2. **Add a Calculated Field:**
   » Go to PivotTable Analyze > Fields, Items & Sets > Calculated Field.
   » Name the field (e.g., "Profit") and enter the formula: ='Sales ($)'- 'Costs ($)'. Note that you have to double-click into the field name in the listed Fields to enter formula.

3. **Customize Calculated Field:**
   » Add the new field to the pivot table.
   » Change the number format for better readability (if needed).

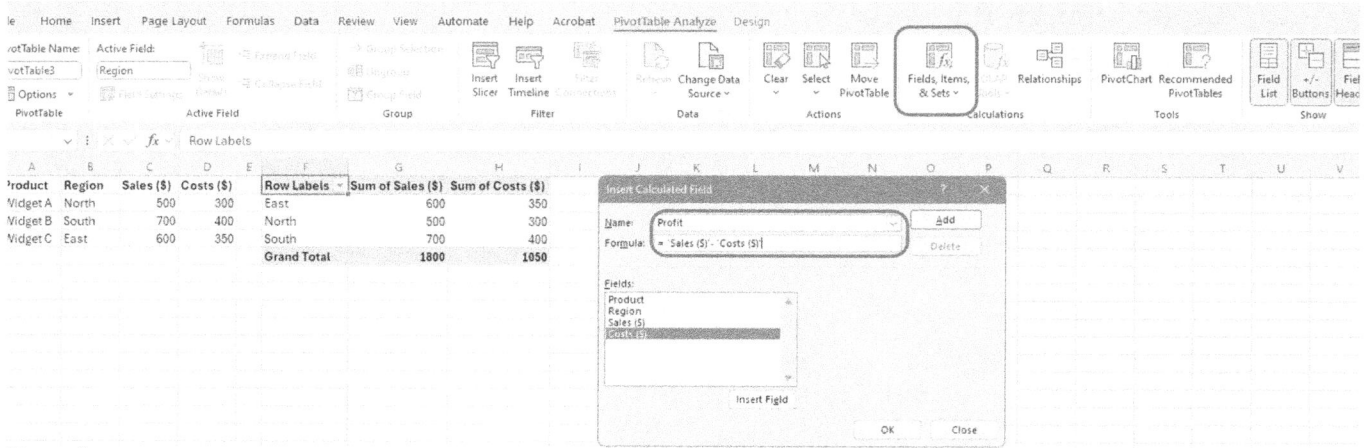

Result:

	A	B	C	D	E	F	G	H	I
1	Product	Region	Sales ($)	Costs ($)		Row Labels	Sum of Sales ($)	Sum of Costs ($)	Sum of Profit
2	Widget A	North	500	300		East	600	350	250
3	Widget B	South	700	400		North	500	300	200
4	Widget C	East	600	350		South	700	400	300
5						Grand Total	1800	1050	750

V.   AUTOMATING TASKS WITH VBA

1.   WHAT IS VBA?

VBA is a programming language integrated into Microsoft Office applications. It allows users to write macros and scripts that automate tasks or add functionality. While macros can be recorded, VBA provides full control to customize and extend Excel's behavior.

Benefits of Using VBA

- **Automation**: Streamline repetitive tasks like formatting, data processing, and report generation.
- **Custom Solutions**: Create tailored tools and features not natively available in Excel.
- **Improved Accuracy**: Reduce manual errors by automating complex workflows.
- **Scalability**: Handle large datasets and advanced tasks with minimal effort.

Key VBA Concepts

- **Variables**: Store data for use in scripts. Example: Dim salesTotal As Double
- **Loops**: Automate repetitive actions. Example: For Each cell In Range("A1:A10")
- **Conditions**: Perform tasks based on criteria. Example: If cell.Value > 250 Then
- **Objects and Methods**: Work with Excel elements like worksheets, ranges, and charts. Example: Worksheets("Sheet1").Range("A1")

Practical Applications of VBA

- **Data Cleanup**: Remove duplicates, format data, and standardize entries.
- **Dynamic Dashboards**: Automate chart updates and slicer interactions.
- **Custom Reports**: Generate reports with consistent formatting and calculations.
- **Bulk Operations**: Apply actions across multiple sheets or files, such as combining data.
- **Interactive Tools**: Create user forms for data entry and analysis.

Tips for Learning and Using VBA

- **Start with the Macro Recorder**: record simple macros and review the generated VBA code to understand syntax.
- **Use Debugging Tools**: use breakpoints and the Immediate Window (Ctrl + G) to test and debug code.
- **Structure Your Code**: use comments (') and modular design to make code readable and maintainable.
- **Leverage Online Resources**: explore forums, tutorials, and documentation for solutions to specific problems.
- **Test on Copies**: run your macros on test files to avoid unintended changes to original data.

2. EXAMPLE: AUTOMATING A SIMPLE TASK

Scenario: Automate the formatting of a sales report.

We have below data in Sheet1 of our workbook.

	A	B	C	D
1	Region	Sales ($)	Costs ($)	Profit ($)
2	North	500	300	200
3	South	700	400	300
4	East	600	350	250
5				

Goal:

- Bold headers.
- Apply currency formatting to numerical values.
- Highlight profits greater than $250.

VBA Code:

```
Sub FormatDataset()
    Dim ws As Worksheet
    Dim dataRange As Range
    Dim headerRange As Range
    Dim profitColumn As Range
    Dim cell As Range
```

```
' Set the worksheet and data range
Set ws = ThisWorkbook.Sheets(1) ' Adjust sheet index if necessary
Set dataRange = ws.Range("A1:D4") ' Adjust range based on your dataset
Set headerRange = ws.Range("A1:D1") ' Adjust header range
Set profitColumn = ws.Range("D2:D4") ' Adjust profit column range

' Bold headers
headerRange.Font.Bold = True

' Apply currency formatting to numerical values
dataRange.Columns("B:D").NumberFormat = "$#,##0"

' Highlight profits greater than $250
For Each cell In profitColumn
    If cell.Value > 250 Then
        cell.Interior.Color = RGB(144, 238, 144) ' Light green color
    End If
Next cell

MsgBox "Formatting applied successfully!", vbInformation
End Sub
```

Explanation of the code:

» **Worksheet and Data Range Setup**: The worksheet is defined as **ws**, and the range containing the dataset is **dataRange**.

» **Bold Headers**: The **headerRange.Font.Bold = True** line applies bold formatting to the headers.

» **Currency Formatting**: The **dataRange.Columns("B:D").NumberFormat = "$#,##0"** line applies currency formatting to the Sales, Costs, and Profit columns.

» **Highlight Profits**:
The **For Each cell In profitColumn** loop checks each value in the Profit column. If the value is greater than $250, the cell is highlighted with a light green color using RGB(144, 238, 144).

» **Success Message**:
A confirmation message (MsgBox) is displayed after the macro is executed.

Steps to Run the Code:

1. Open the **VBA Editor**: Press Alt + F11.
2. Insert a new module: **Insert > Module**.
3. Paste the code into the module.
4. Close the editor and return to Excel.
5. Run the macro: Press Alt + F8, select FormatDataset, and click **Run**.

Result:

	Region	Sales ($)	Costs ($)	Profit ($)
1				
2	North	$500	$300	$200
3	South	$700	$400	$300
4	East	$600	$350	$250

Microsoft Excel

Formatting applied successfully!

OK

VI. INTRODUCTION TO POWER PIVOT FOR LARGE DATASETS

Power Pivot is an advanced data modeling and analysis tool in Excel that enables you to work with large datasets, create relationships between data tables, and perform complex calculations efficiently. It extends Excel's capabilities by leveraging the power of a built-in database engine and the DAX (Data Analysis Expressions) language.

1. WHAT IS POWER PIVOT?

Power Pivot is an Excel add-in designed for advanced data analysis. It allows you to create data models, establish relationships, and create calculations. With Power Pivot you can work with large data sets, build extensive relationships, and create complex (or simple) calculations, all in a high-performance environment, and all within the familiar experience of Excel.

Key Features:

- Handle large datasets beyond Excel's row limit.
- Create relationships between tables without using **VLOOKUP**.
- Use DAX formulas for complex calculations.
- Build efficient, memory-optimized data models.

Use Cases for Power Pivot

- **Combining Data from Multiple Sources**: import data from SQL databases, Excel files, and web services into a single model.

- **Complex Relationships**: build relationships between tables without flattening data into one worksheet.
- **Advanced Reporting**: create interactive dashboards with calculated fields and advanced metrics.
- **Handling Large Data**: analyze millions of rows without performance issues.

2. ENABLING POWER PIVOT

Power Pivot is available in Excel for Microsoft 365, Excel 2024, Excel 2021, Excel 2019, and Excel 2016. To enable it:

1. Go to **File > Options > Add-Ins**.
2. Under **Manage**, select **COM Add-ins** and click **Go**.
3. Check **Microsoft Power Pivot for Excel** and click **OK**.

3. STEPS TO USE POWER PIVOT

Step 1: Import Data

- Open Power Pivot: Go to **Power Pivot > Manage**.
- Import data from multiple sources: Excel files, databases, web data, etc.

Step 2: Create Relationships

- In the Power Pivot window, go to **Diagram View**.
- Drag and drop fields to establish relationships between tables (e.g., link ProductID in the Sales table to ProductID in the Product table).

Step 3: Add Calculations Using DAX

- Use DAX formulas to create calculated fields, columns, and measures.

Step 4: Build Pivot Tables and Charts

- Close the Power Pivot window. Then insert a PivotTable in Excel using **Insert > PivotTable > From Data Model**; or
- Within the Power Pivot window, select PivotTable > New Worksheet.

4. EXAMPLE: ANALYZING SALES DATA WITH POWER PIVOT

Scenario: Combine sales data from multiple tables to analyze total sales by region and product.

We have Sales table and Products table in 2 sheets in our workbook.

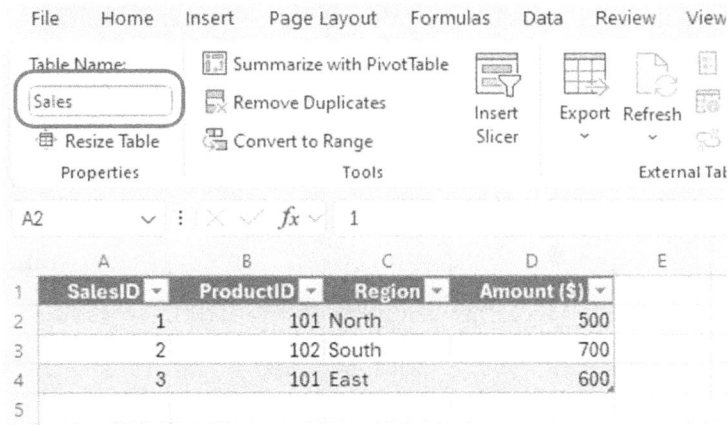
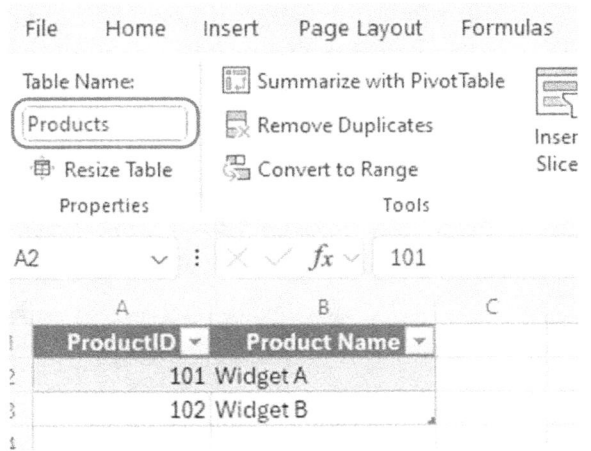

Steps:

1. Go to the Power Pivot tab in Excel and click Manage to open the Power Pivot window

2. In the Power Pivot window:

   » Click Home → From Other Sources → Excel File.

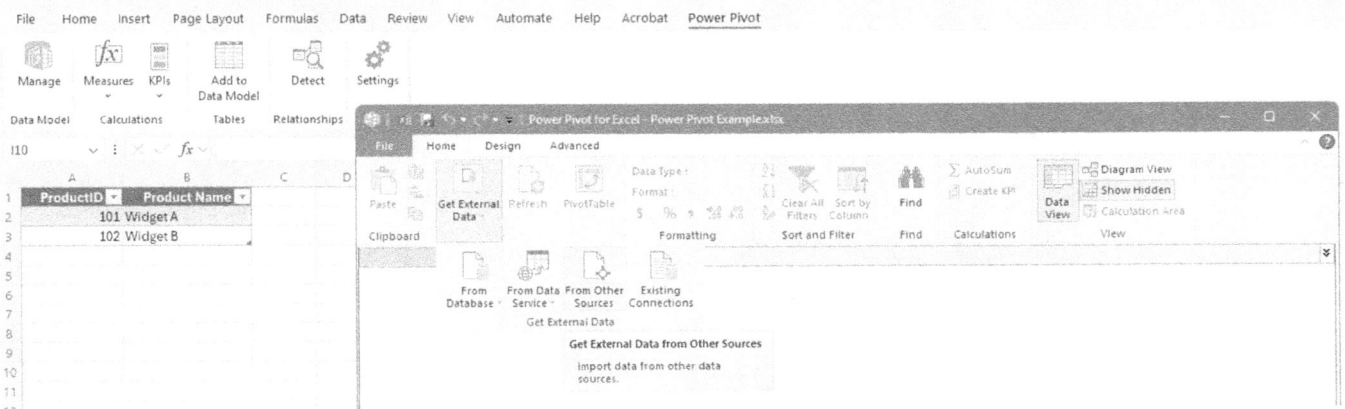

   » Browse to the current workbook and select it.

   » Check both Sales and Products tables for import and click Next.

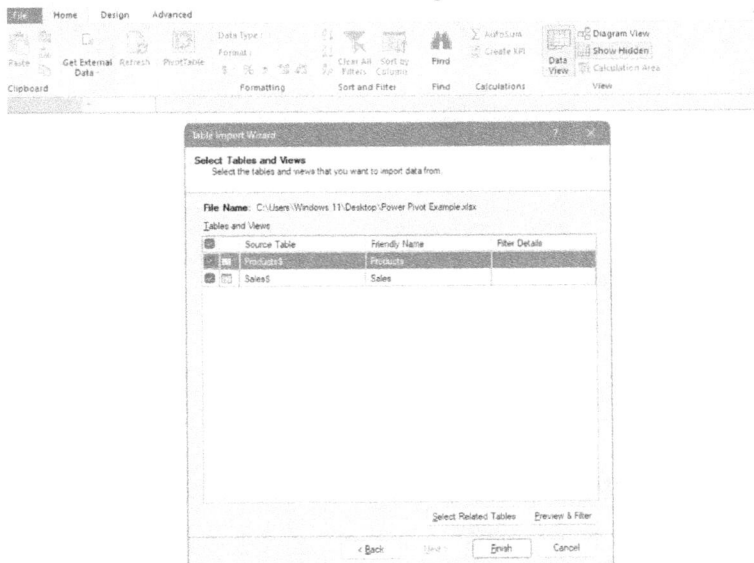

» Rename tables if needed and click Finish. The data from both tables will now be loaded into Power Pivot.

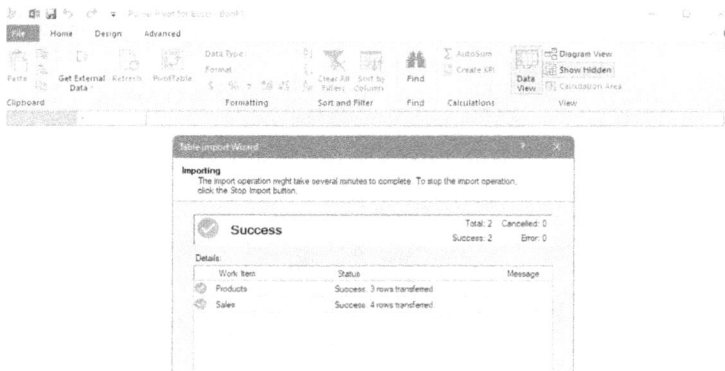

3. In the Power Pivot window, go to the Diagram View (button on the top-right). Drag the ProductID column from the Sales table to the ProductID column in the Products table.

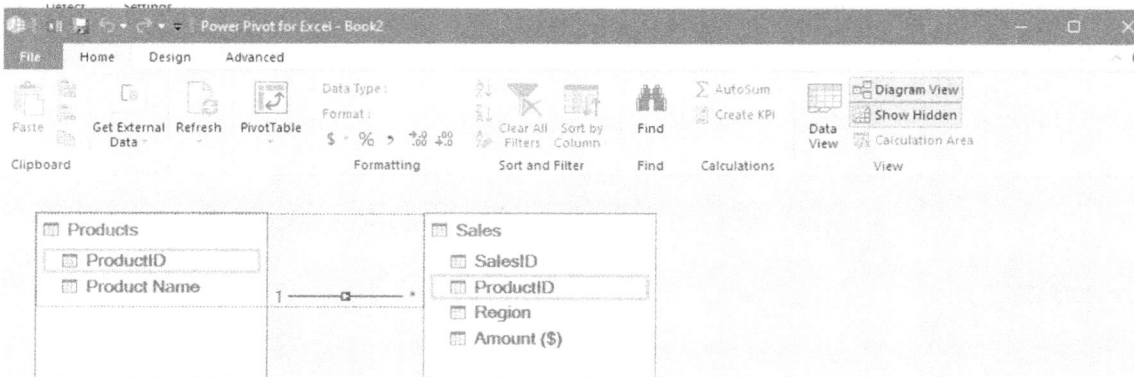

4. Add a calculated field for total sales and rename the header of that column as Total Sales.

5. In the Power Pivot window, click on PivotTable to build a PivotTable to display sales by region and product.

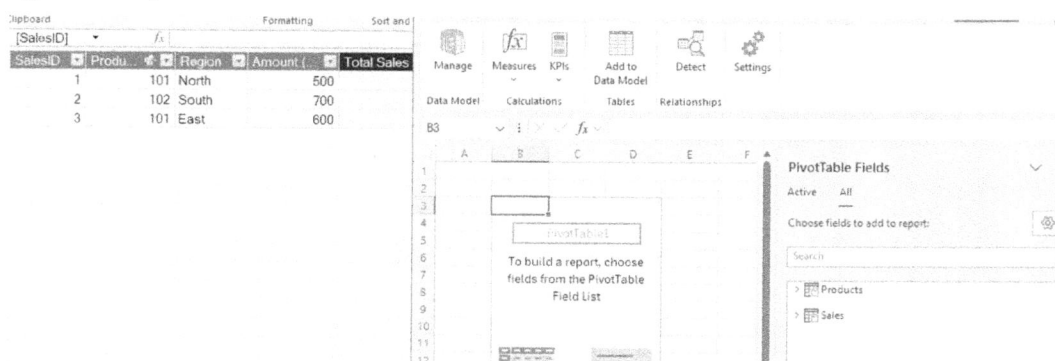

6. In the PivotTable Field List:

   » Drag Region (from the Sales table) to the Rows area.

   » Drag Product Name (from the Products table) to the Columns area.

   » Drag Amount ($) (from the Sales table) to the Values area.

   » This will display the total sales amount for each region and product.

Sum of Amount ($)	Column Labels		
Row Labels	Widget A	Widget B	Grand Total
East	600		600
North	500		500
South		700	700
Grand Total	1100	700	1800

Result:

Sum of Amount ($)	Column Labels		
Row Labels	Widget A	Widget B	Grand Total
East	600		600
North	500		500
South		700	700
Grand Total	1100	700	1800

5. ADVANCED FEATURES IN POWER PIVOT

- **Hierarchies**: create hierarchies (e.g., Year > Quarter > Month) for intuitive reporting.
- **KPI (Key Performance Indicators)**: define KPIs using measures and thresholds to track performance.
- **Data Views**: use **Diagram View** to visualize relationships and **Data View** for editing tables.
- **Time Intelligence**: use DAX functions like TOTALYTD, SAMEPERIODLASTYEAR, or DATEADD for time-based analysis.

6. PRACTICAL TIPS FOR USING POWER PIVOT

- **Use Clean Data**: ensure source data is clean and formatted before importing.
- **Optimize Relationships**: avoid unnecessary relationships to improve performance.
- **Leverage Measures**: use measures instead of calculated columns for better efficiency in large datasets.
- **Combine with Power Query**: use Power Query for data transformation before loading into Power Pivot.

CHAPTER 8: COLLABORATION AND CLOUD INTEGRATION

I.   SHARING WORKBOOKS WITH ONEDRIVE

Sharing workbooks via OneDrive simplifies collaboration by enabling access from anywhere, ensuring all users work on the most up-to-date version of the file.

1.   WHY USE ONEDRIVE FOR SHARING?

Accessibility: Access files from any device connected to the internet.

Real-Time Updates: Changes are saved and synced instantly, reducing version conflicts.

Security: Manage permissions to control who can view or edit your workbooks.

2.   STEPS TO SHARE WORKBOOKS WITH ONEDRIVE

Save Workbook to OneDrive:

>   » Go to **File > Save As** and select **OneDrive** as the location.

Share the Workbook:

>   » Click **Share** in the top-right corner of Excel.
>
>   » Enter email addresses of collaborators or copy the link to share.
>
>   » Set permissions: Choose **Can Edit** or **Can View** based on the collaborator's role.

Access Sharing Settings:

>   » Click **Manage Access** to update permissions or stop sharing.

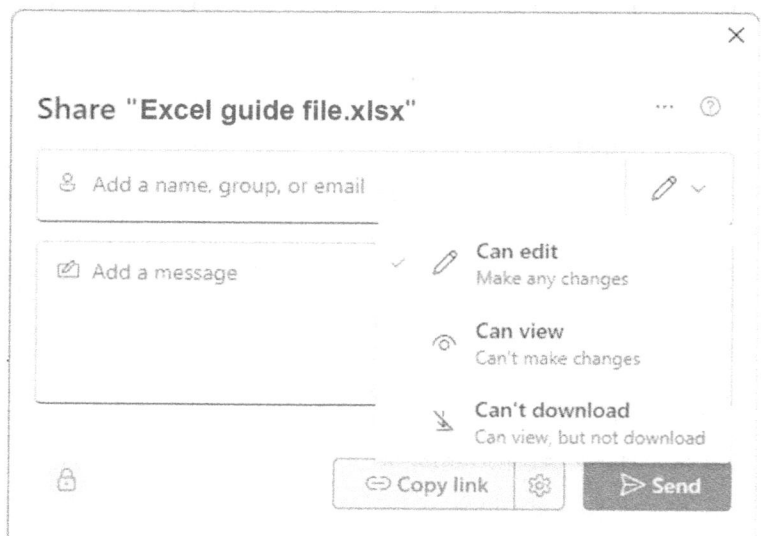

Chapter 8 - Figure 11.   Share a Workbook.png

II.   CO-EDITING IN REAL-TIME

Real-time co-editing allows multiple users to work simultaneously on the same workbook, enhancing productivity and reducing delays in collaborative tasks.

1. BENEFITS OF REAL-TIME CO-EDITING

Increased Efficiency: No need to wait for others to complete their changes.

Instant Updates: Changes appear in real-time for all collaborators.

Version Control: One shared file eliminates the need for multiple versions.

2. STEPS TO ENABLE REAL-TIME CO-EDITING

1. **Save Workbook to OneDrive or SharePoint**: ensure the workbook is stored in a shared cloud location.
2. **Share the Workbook**:
   » Click **Share** in the top-right corner.
   » Set permissions to **Can Edit** for collaborators.
3. **Collaborate in Real-Time**: when collaborators open the shared workbook, their presence is indicated by colored flags or initials on the cells they are editing.

3. ADDING AND MANAGING COMMENTS

Add a Comment: right-click a cell and select **New Comment** to open the comment thread.

Reply to Comments: collaborators can reply directly in the comment thread for easy discussion.

Resolve or Delete Comments: once a discussion is completed, mark the comment as resolved or delete it.

III. LINKING EXCEL WITH WORD, POWERPOINT, AND TEAMS

Integrating Excel with other Microsoft tools like Word, PowerPoint, and Teams enhances productivity by streamlining workflows and enabling seamless sharing of data across platforms.

1. LINKING EXCEL WITH WORD

Linking Excel to Word allows you to embed or link data for reports or documents that require dynamic updates.

Use Cases:

- Creating reports with live Excel tables and charts.
- Embedding financial summaries or data snapshots.

Steps:

- **Copy and Paste as a Linked Object:**
  - » In Excel, copy the desired range (e.g., a table or chart).
  - » In Word, use **Paste Special > Paste Link** to link the data dynamically.
  - » Updates in the Excel file reflect automatically in Word.

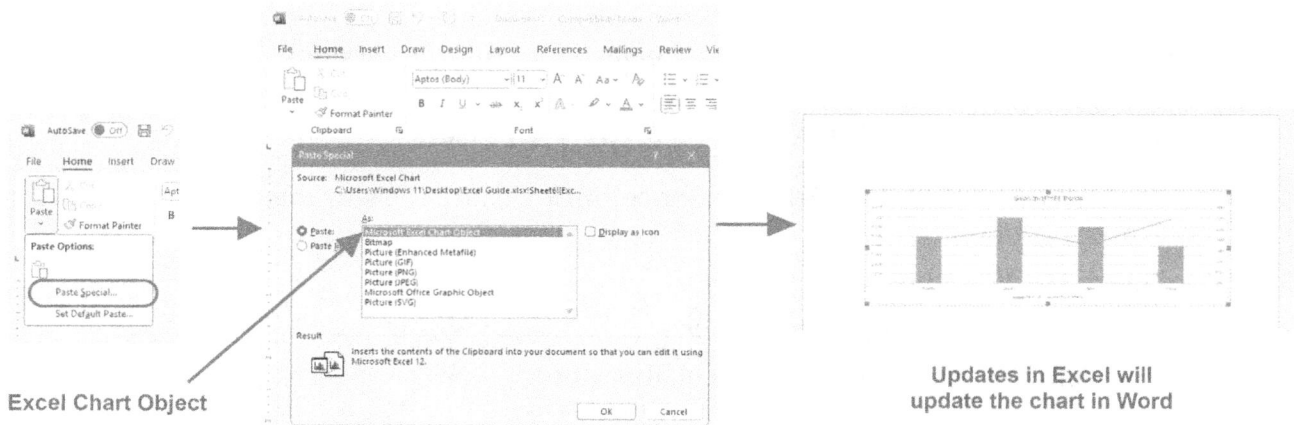

Chapter 8 - Figure 12.   Linked Object with Word.png

- **Embed as a Static Object:**
  - » Copy the range from Excel and paste it into Word as a static table or image.
  - » Use this for documents that don't require updates.

- **Insert Excel Workbook as an Object:**
  - » In Word, go to **Insert > Object > Create from File**, and select your Excel workbook.
  - » Choose **Link to file** for dynamic updates or leave it unchecked for a static version.

2.   LINKING EXCEL WITH POWERPOINT

Excel's integration with PowerPoint is ideal for presentations requiring live or formatted data visualizations.

Use Cases:

- Displaying charts and graphs in presentations.
- Updating tables in PowerPoint automatically when Excel data changes.

Steps:

- **Copy and Paste as a Linked Object:**
  - » Copy an Excel chart or table.
  - » In PowerPoint, use **Paste Special > Paste Link**.
  - » Updates in the Excel file are reflected in PowerPoint.

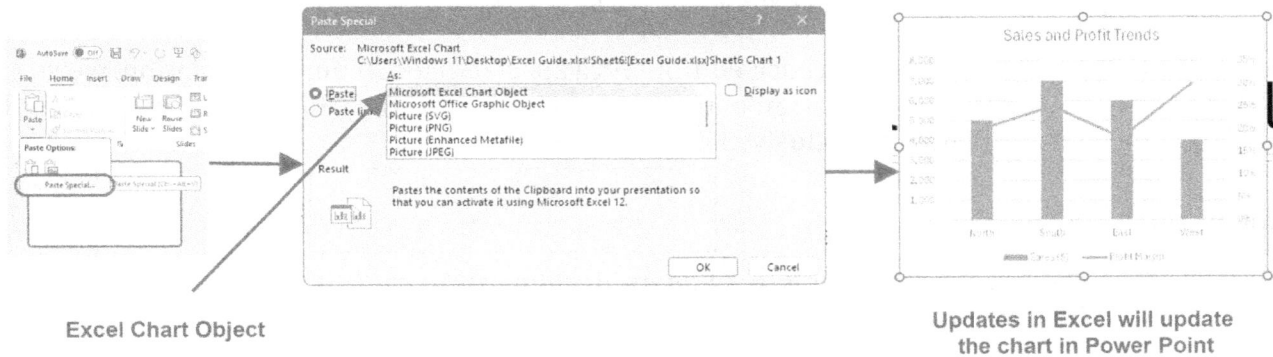

Excel Chart Object

Updates in Excel will update
the chart in Power Point

Chapter 8 - Figure 13.   Linked Object with PowerPoint.png

- **Embed Excel Data:**
  - » Insert the Excel file as an object using **Insert > Object > Create from File**.
  - » Double-clicking the embedded file opens it for editing.

- **Use Export Options:**
  - » In Excel, format your data and export it directly to PowerPoint using **File > Export > Create Handouts**.

3. LINKING EXCEL WITH TEAMS

Microsoft Teams integrates seamlessly with Excel for collaborative editing and sharing of workbooks in real-time.

Use Cases:

- » Collaborating on shared workbooks during Teams meetings.
- » Sharing dynamic dashboards or reports.

Steps:

- **Share an Excel Workbook in Teams:**
  - » Upload your workbook to a Teams channel or chat using **Files > Upload**.
  - » Click the uploaded file to open it directly in Teams for editing.

- **Collaborate in Real-Time:**
  - » Multiple users can edit the workbook simultaneously in Teams or open it in Excel Online.

- **Pin Excel Files for Quick Access:**
  - » Pin important workbooks to the channel tab for easy access by team members.

- **Use Excel During Meetings:**
  - » Share the Excel workbook live in a Teams meeting using **Share Screen** or by opening it in the meeting chat.

BONUS CONTENT

Thank you for purchasing the paperback edition! As a special token of our appreciation, we're excited to offer you a free eBook version of this guide. Simply scan the QR code below to access the eBook on any device and unlock exclusive bonus content:

Your Exclusive Bonuses:

1. 20+ Ready-to-Use Templates — budgets, dashboards, project planners, invoice trackers & more (instant download)
2. Exclusive ChatGPT & Copilot Guide — supercharge formulas, cleaning, analysis & automation with simple prompts
3. Excel Shortcuts Cheatsheet — time-saving keys pros rely on every day
4. Video Tips Library — bite-sized walkthroughs for every skill level
5. Practice Exercises + Solutions — learn by doing and self-check instantly
6. New! Monthly Template Drops — join our readers' club for fresh resources all year

Take your Excel skills to the next level with these additional resources. Enjoy exploring!

CHAPTER 9:
TROUBLESHOOTING AND FAQS

I.   HOW TO CHECK A FORMULA

Formulas are the backbone of Excel, but errors in long or complex formulas can be hard to spot. By leveraging Excel's built-in tools and features, you can ensure accuracy and quickly resolve issues.

1.   STEPS TO CHECK A FORMULA

Double-Check Formula Syntax:
  - » Ensure the formula starts with an equal sign (=).
  - » Confirm all parentheses are properly balanced.

Use Formula Auditing Tools: navigate to **Formulas > Formula Auditing**:
  - » **Trace Precedents**: Identify cells contributing to the formula.
  - » **Trace Dependents**: Highlight cells affected by the formula.
  - » **Error Checking**: Locate and resolve issues within the formula.

Evaluate Formula Step-by-Step:
  - » Go to **Formulas > Evaluate Formula**.
  - » View intermediate results of each calculation within the formula.

Preview Results of Formula Parts (Using F9):
  - » **Highlight a Part of the Formula**: In the formula bar, select a specific section (e.g., a nested function or a range reference).
  - » **Press F9**: Displays the result of the selected part.
  - » **Undo (Ctrl + Z)**: Reverts the preview to the original formula.

2.   EXAMPLE: CHECKING A LONG FORMULA

Scenario: Calculate Total Profit from multiple regions:

=SUM(Sales_North, Sales_South, Sales_East) - SUM(Exp_North, ExpSouth, Exp_East)

Steps to Debug:

1. **Trace Precedents**:
   » Use **Trace Precedents** to confirm the correct ranges (Sales_North, Expenses_South, etc.) are linked.

2. **Evaluate the Formula**:
   » Open **Evaluate Formula** to review step-by-step calculations, ensuring correct intermediate results.

3. **Use F9 for Quick Validation**:
   » Highlight SUM(Sales_North, Sales_South, Sales_East) in the formula bar.
   » Press **F9** to see the total sales (e.g., $50,000).
   » Highlight SUM(Exp_North, Exp_South, Exp_East) and press **F9** to see the total expenses (e.g., $30,000).
   » Ensure the difference (profit) matches expectations.
   » Press **Ctrl + Z** after each F9 action to restore the original formula.

II. COMMON ERRORS AND HOW TO FIX THEM (#DIV/0!, #VALUE!, #NAME?)

Excel formulas can produce error messages when something goes wrong. Understanding the causes and solutions for these errors ensures smooth workflows and accurate results.

1. COMMON EXCEL ERRORS AND THEIR FIXES

i.   #DIV/0!

Cause: Division by zero or a blank cell in the denominator.

Solution:
   » Check the denominator for zero or blanks.
   » Use an error-handling formula: =IF(B1=0, "Error: Division by Zero", A1/B1); or use the IFERROR function.

ii.   #VALUE!

Cause: A formula includes incompatible data types (e.g., text in a numeric calculation).

Solution:
   » Verify that all inputs are numbers where required.
   » Use the VALUE() function to convert text to numbers if needed.

iii. #REF!

Cause: A formula refers to a deleted or invalid cell or range.

Solution:

> » Avoid deleting cells or ranges used in formulas.
> » Update formulas to reference valid cells or ranges.

iv. #NAME?

Cause: A misspelled function name or undefined named range.

Solution:

> » Verify the formula for typos in function names.
> » Ensure named ranges are properly defined.

v. #N/A

Cause: A lookup function (e.g., VLOOKUP or HLOOKUP) cannot find the specified value.

Solution:

> » Confirm that the lookup value exists in the search range.
> » Use =IFNA(VLOOKUP(...), "Not Found") to handle errors gracefully.

vi. #NUM!

Cause: Invalid numeric operations (e.g., square root of a negative number).

Solution:

> » Validate input values before performing calculations.
> » Use logical functions like IF to handle special cases.

2. TOOLS FOR ERROR RESOLUTION

Error Checking: go to **Formulas > Error Checking** to identify and resolve errors step-by-step.

Trace Precedents and Dependents: use these tools to locate cells contributing to or affected by an error.

Evaluate Formula: break down formulas into components to identify where the error occurs.

III. TIPS FOR SPEEDING UP SLOW EXCEL WORKBOOKS

Large datasets, complex formulas, and heavy formatting can cause Excel workbooks to slow down. By following optimization techniques and best practices, you can significantly improve performance and maintain efficiency.

1. IDENTIFY PERFORMANCE BOTTLENECKS

Check File Size:
>   » Go to **File > Info** to review the workbook size.
>   » Large files (>10 MB) often cause delays.

Review Complex Formulas:
>   » Identify and optimize nested or array formulas.

Monitor Performance:
>   » Use **Task Manager** (Windows) or **Activity Monitor** (Mac) to identify if Excel is using excessive system resources.

2. TIPS FOR IMPROVING WORKBOOK SPEED

i. Optimize Formulas

Avoid Volatile Functions:
>   » Functions like NOW(), TODAY(), and INDIRECT() recalculate with every change, slowing performance. Use them sparingly.

Use Helper Columns:
>   » Break complex calculations into smaller, intermediate steps for efficiency.

Minimize Array Formulas:
>   » Replace array formulas with simpler alternatives when possible.

ii. Save in Binary Format

Why Use Binary Format (.xlsb)?
>   » Binary workbooks are smaller and load faster because they are optimized for storage and speed. This reduces file size significantly without losing functionality, especially for workbooks with large datasets or complex formulas.

How to Save in Binary Format:

> » Go to **File > Save As**.
> » In the **Save as type** dropdown, select **Excel Binary Workbook (.xlsb)**.
> » Save your file.

iii. Reduce Workbook Size

Delete Unused Data:
> » Remove blank rows, columns, and worksheets.

Compress Images:
> » If your workbook contains images, use **File > Compress Pictures** to reduce their size.

Clear Excessive Formatting:
> » Select the range and click **Clear > Clear Formats** to remove unnecessary borders, colors, and styles.

iv. Optimize Data Connections

Limit External Links:
> » Replace links to other workbooks with imported or static data.

Cache Data Locally:
> » Use **Power Query** to cache large datasets instead of repeatedly querying external sources.

v. Manage Workbook Calculations

Switch to Manual Calculation Mode:
> » Go to **Formulas > Calculation Options > Manual**.
> » Press **F9** to recalculate only when necessary.

Group Large Calculations:
> » Divide large calculations into smaller ranges to process incrementally.

vi. Streamline Pivot Tables

- **Disable Auto Refresh**: refresh pivot tables manually to avoid unnecessary recalculations.
- **Filter Data at the Source**: reduce the size of pivot tables by pre-filtering the data source.

IV. PROTECTING YOUR DATA: BACKUPS AND RECOVERY

Data loss is a significant risk when working with Excel, especially with complex workbooks. Understanding how to create backups and recover data ensures your work is always secure.

1. CREATING BACKUPS IN EXCEL

Use the AutoSave Feature:

> » Available in Excel for Microsoft 365.
> » Enable **AutoSave** in the top-left corner to automatically save changes to your OneDrive or SharePoint files.

Save Backup Copies Manually:

> » Go to **File > Save As > More Options > Tools > General Options**.
> » Check **Always create backup** before saving.

Version History:

> » If your workbook is stored on OneDrive or SharePoint, you can access previous versions.
> » Go to **File > Info > Version History** to view or restore older versions.

Use External Storage:

> » Save important files to external drives or cloud services like Google Drive or Dropbox.

2. RECOVERING UNSAVED WORKBOOKS

Recover from AutoRecover:

> » Go to **File > Info > Manage Workbook > Recover Unsaved Workbooks**.
> » Select the file and click **Open** to restore.

Recover from Temporary Files:

> » If Excel crashes, reopen the application. Look for files in the **Document Recovery Pane**.

Check Backup Files:

> » If you enabled backups, locate the .xls backup file in the same folder as your original workbook.

CONCLUSION

Congratulations on completing this comprehensive Excel guide! You've unlocked a powerful toolkit, from mastering the basics to applying advanced techniques, enabling you to tackle a wide range of personal, professional, and business challenges. Excel isn't just a spreadsheet program—it's a gateway to smarter decisions, streamlined workflows, and impactful insights.

As you continue your journey, remember that every click, formula, and function brings you closer to becoming an Excel expert. Keep exploring, experimenting, and applying what you've learned. With the skills and strategies in this book, you're well-equipped to transform data into knowledge and opportunities.

Excel is more than a tool—it's your ally in achieving excellence. Happy excelling!

ABOUT THE AUTHOR

Ethan Wells is a seasoned finance and accounting professional with over 14 years of experience in auditing, corporate finance, financial management, and strategic consulting. After building a strong foundation in global corporations, Ethan transitioned into a pivotal consulting role, helping startups and innovative ventures achieve sustainable growth and financial success.

Driven by a passion for simplifying complex financial topics, Ethan writes practical, easy-to-understand guides designed for entrepreneurs, business owners, and professionals. His approachable style, combined with deep industry expertise, empowers readers to confidently navigate the evolving landscape of business, finance, and accounting.

Explore more titles in the Business Productivity Blueprint series to continue building your skills and boosting your productivity. From mastering Excel and Word to managing your business with QuickBooks and Office 365, there's a guide for every step of your journey.